3-20-21

John
I know it's deep
for young mothers. But
I thought you might like—

love you
mom

D1116007

365 Pocket® Prayers for Mothers
Guidance and Wisdom for Each New Day

AMIE CARLSON
KAREN HODGE
ERIN KEELEY MARSHALL

Tyndale House Publishers, Inc. Carol Stream, Illinois

Visit Tyndale online at www.tyndale.com.

TYNDALE, Tyndale's quill logo, *365 Pocket*, and *LeatherLike* are
registered trademarks of Tyndale House Publishers, Inc.

365 Pocket Prayers for Mothers: Guidance and Wisdom for Each New Day

Designed by Jennifer Phelps

Published in association with The Livingstone Corporation.

ISBN 978-1-4143-9039-0

Printed in China

20 19 18 17 16 15 14
7   6   5   4   3   2   1

INTRODUCTION

Becoming a mother changes us. Whether our children are eighteen months or eighteen years old, they are often first in our thoughts when we wake up and the last thing on our minds at bedtime.

No matter how old our children are, the best source for parenting wisdom, comfort, and relief is prayer. Prayer is simply talking with God. It is turning over our concerns, our struggles, and our questions to him. As women of faith, we can come to him anytime, approach him anywhere, and pray about anything. God loves our honest, heartfelt prayers, and he cares deeply for the details of our lives.

Perhaps your faith is relatively new and you're not yet comfortable praying. This book is for you. The prayers we've developed can be claimed as your own conversations with God. As you pray through each topic and day, we hope you will become more comfortable talking with God and will even begin to form your own prayers to him.

Perhaps you've been a believer for years but need a little inspiration in your prayer life. This book is for you, too. If discouragement or fear for your children sometimes makes it difficult to find the right words, these prayers may allow you to express your concerns in a new way. By including a year's worth of unique prayers that cover a broad range of topics, this book will help rejuvenate your dialogue with God.

Thank God that we don't have to be spiritually mature or "on fire" to have a meaningful prayer life! Wherever you are in your spiritual journey, God is delighted when you draw near to him. We hope this little book will help you do so.

You will find 365 prayers, arranged by days and topics.

You can pray through each day of the year consecutively if you wish. Alternatively, look in the index for a topic that will help you pray through an urgent need or give words to something you may be experiencing. Every few days you will also find prayers called *Prayerful Moments*. These are shorter prayers for days when time is limited or for when you need a quick word with God.

As you enter into a new prayer, take it slow. Spend some time thinking about what you're saying to God, and try to personalize each prayer for your own life and child. Making each written prayer your own honest praise or petition will make it more meaningful.

In your conversations with God, take some time to listen. Reading God's Word as a part of your prayer time gives the Lord an opportunity to speak to you, too. We've included a Scripture verse at the end of each prayer to help you ponder what God might be communicating to you.

By the time you reach the end of this book, we hope you will be inspired in your conversations with God and—most important—feel closer to him than ever before. It is often in these special times of prayer that God does his powerful work in our hearts. So don't give up; stick with it. As his Word says to us, "Let us come boldly to the throne of our gracious God. There we will receive his mercy, and we will find grace to help us when we need it most" (Hebrews 4:16).

The privilege of prayer is that it ushers us straight into the presence of our loving God. And Scripture promises us that he won't disappoint! With that in mind, it's time to begin.

☀ **A prayer about HOPE**
 When I need perspective

LORD,

Remembering the day I watched my child take her first wobbly steps into my arms reminds me of how you have promised to be there with me as I take steps of faith into the unknown future. Like her, I am not always steady on my feet. I am so thankful that you have not left me here to walk this journey alone. You are right here with me.

Thank you for never leaving me and for using the memory of my little child to show me a glimpse of the hope that comes from a future with you. Thank you for working everything I do together for your purpose. Help me to seek your will in my life.

We are merely moving shadows, and all our busy rushing ends in nothing. We heap up wealth, not knowing who will spend it. And so, Lord, where do I put my hope? My only hope is in you. PSALM 39:6-7

☼ A prayer about CHILDREN
When I realize how much they teach me

LORD,

I knew that children are blessings from you, but I really had no idea how often they'd gift me with lessons I've needed to learn for a long time. Their innocence inspires me to trust you more; their giggles prompt me to choose joy; their sense of adventure encourages me to live fully. Through them I'm learning to jump, to take the risks of wholehearted devotion to you and those I love. When I observe them, I'm reminded that I can help other little ones in need. They remind me to be thankful to you for providing for our needs and to live with a giving heart.

Father, how many children on this earth aren't appreciated? They all have so much promise, so much to learn, and even more to teach. Open my eyes ever wider to look for ways I can minister to the children you place in my life. Thank you for them, Lord. I would not be the same without them, and I'm not done growing through them.

The disciples came to Jesus and asked, "Who is greatest in the Kingdom of Heaven?" Jesus called a little child to him and put the child among them. MATTHEW 18:1-2

☼ A prayer about TRUST
When I am looking for an easier way

HEAVENLY FATHER,

As we sit around the coffee shop and chat, I am amazed by my friends' strategies and plans to produce successful children. I too have been lured by the tendency to follow a simple ten-step methodology. But I wonder if an easy prescriptive formula for raising healthy kids is even possible. Will I place my trust in the best academics for their future? Perhaps I will center my attention on developing their gifts, talents, and abilities. Even though I am tempted to use a worldly approach to parenting, I know deep down that those foundations are shaky at best.

I repent of my misplaced trust in the methods of this world. I have invested far too much time, energy, and resources and received far too little in return. I do not want what the world says is best for my children but rather what you have shown me is eternally the best. I want my children to live in a manner that pleases you. Give me grace to trust them and their futures to what you say in your Word.

Some nations boast of their chariots and horses, but we boast in the name of the LORD our God. PSALM 20:7

☼ A prayer about DISTRACTIONS
When I long to be fully attentive to you

FATHER,

I long to be distracted. By you, that is. I'm distracted more often than focused, it seems, but not often by what's most valuable. Instead of thinking of you off and on between the many other things vying for my attention, I'd like to flip those habits around and make you my great distraction.

Will you interrupt anything that threatens to draw me away from you? Interrupt any dream that is not from you and replace it with your best for me. And if I begin to believe any line of thinking that doesn't honor you, stop me in my tracks—whatever it takes. Fill me with the concerns that fill your heart. Flood me with the reality of yourself. Bathe me with your presence and glory. Be my number one priority, my favorite pastime, my most cherished relationship, my most passionate longing, my complete fulfillment, my only Lord, and my life's meaning. Today and forever, will you give "distraction" new meaning and be my greatest one?

Those who are controlled by the Holy Spirit think about things that please the Spirit. ROMANS 8:5

⚙ **A prayer about JEALOUSY**
When my child envies others

LORD,

The teenage years can be challenging and hurtful. Watching my child struggle with envy and comparison as she navigates the awkward, painful years of puberty reminds me how important it is to root my identity in you.

You created each and every one of your children to have individual strengths and talents. No person is exactly like another by design, so that everyone can contribute to the world in a unique way. Remind me to point out that her abilities—the ones she so often claims are nothing special—are gifts from you designed to brighten her life and those of everyone around her. Help me to affirm my child so that she knows she is beautiful just the way she is and doesn't need to be like anyone else. Thank you for loving her and for walking with her through the challenges of these years.

See how very much our Father loves us, for he calls us his children, and that is what we are! 1 JOHN 3:1

☼ **A prayer about REGRETS**
   When I feel troubled about the past

GOD,

Tonight I feel nearly paralyzed by my past mistakes and sins. Consequences of my poor choices and decisions continue to ripple through my life today. I lay my sins at your feet, asking you to cleanse me and to cast them as far as the east is from the west, just as you promise in your Word. Then help me to rest, knowing that tomorrow will be a new opportunity to forsake the past and look forward to the future.

No, dear brothers and sisters, I have not achieved it, but I focus on this one thing: Forgetting the past and looking forward to what lies ahead. PHILIPPIANS 3:13

DAY 7 *Prayerful Moment*

☼ **A prayer about the POWER OF GOD**
   When I stand in awe

GOD,

I marvel at your majesty and creation. You are aware of the tiniest details, from the perfectly shaped fingernails on my tiny baby to the vivid colors of every sunset. I am so proud to call you my heavenly Father. Please give me the boldness to tell someone about your matchless power today.

O Sovereign LORD! You made the heavens and earth by your strong hand and powerful arm. Nothing is too hard for you! JEREMIAH 32:17

DAY 8

☼ **A prayer about ENVY**
When I feel it shrink my heart

LORD,

Your Word says that jealousy leads to evil of *every* kind. Really? I know envy feels awful, but to think that all other evils play on the same playground as jealousy—wow. That puts a new spin on the need to get rid of it at all costs. Whenever I feel envy's bite, I find that my ability to be a solid friend shrinks. I also feel my attractiveness fade. Absolutely nothing good comes from feeling negatively about the blessings others enjoy. I want to be good and healthy, for my own spirit as well as for others.

So Father, I'm committing to a zero-tolerance approach to envy in my life. I know it will bare its fangs again because I'm human. But when it does, please sharpen my weapons to fight back. Please help me turn the negative emotions into strength to battle and win with the truth that I am blessedly yours. You make me thrive when I'm focused on you. Help me go deeper with you until I can cheer without reservation for others, even if I don't have the same gifts in my life. And Lord, I trust that obeying you in this will result in rich blessings in my heart and relationships.

Wherever there is jealousy and selfish ambition, there you will find disorder and evil of every kind. JAMES 3:16

☀ **A prayer about BALANCE**
When the world has me doubting the value of hope

FATHER,

Sometimes I get cynical about life because the world is so mixed up. When society is geared to pulling my family away from you, I don't feel very gracious toward those who demean you and your own. Sometimes I forget that my hope is in you, not in humanity or this earthly existence. But God, if I stick to your truth yet allow my heart to be tainted by resentment toward those who fight you but still need you, then I have a problem. I won't draw others to you by appearing hopeless. This world needs to see lives transformed by you, and I want to be one of those lives.

Will you please help me to balance living with eyes wide open and reflecting your gracious heart of hope so I won't waste my energy with cynicism? If my hope really is in you and not in this shaky life, then I can hold to your truth with a gracious heart.

Let all that I am wait quietly before God, for my hope is in him. PSALM 62:5

☼ A prayer about honoring our PARENTS
When I fail to consider those who gave me life

FATHER,

Forgive me when my words are short and my patience is even shorter in dealing with my parents. Many times I am overcome with their neediness and desire to monopolize my time. Yet I am convicted by the hours upon hours they spent caring for me. They extended patience even when I took it for granted. They generously provided for my needs and many of my wants.

Give me grace to consider their needs as more important than my own. Show me creative ways to care for their needs as Christ has cared for mine. Help me to remember that I am modeling for my own children what it means to honor their parents in the very ways I choose to neglect or honor my own parents. May I seek to honor your Word in this matter. In doing so, I will inevitably honor my father and mother too. Thank you, Lord, that this command leads to a promise. This is a promise I long for—that you would give me a life that is rich, full, and overflowing with blessings from your generous hand.

Honor your father and mother. Then you will live a long, full life in the land the LORD your God is giving you.
EXODUS 20:12

✦ **A prayer about LOYALTY**
When I sin again

LORD,

Even when I continually ignore you and sin against you, you continually forgive me and bless my life. I can't even begin to fathom that kind of loyalty. I get a small glimpse of it when my child throws a fit or treats me badly. Love really does overcome all wrongs. Teach me, by following your example and by the power of your Spirit, to be forgiving, loyal, and dependable in the midst of difficult circumstances.

Help me teach my children the value of loyalty and forgiveness rather than holding grudges when they are wronged. I pray that they will learn early to look to you for the grace they need to be merciful to those who have let them down. Thank you for the gift of forgiveness, and thank you for never walking away from me or my children.

He is the Rock; his deeds are perfect. Everything he does is just and fair. He is a faithful God who does no wrong; how just and upright he is! DEUTERONOMY 32:4

☀ **A prayer about SURPRISE**
When I am far too easily impressed

LORD,

I fear as a family we have amused ourselves to death. Most days the mundane aspects of life far too easily impress us. At other times we are lulled into a dull stupor by the monotony of life. But thank you, dear Lord, that you liberate us from our complacent thinking. Tonight you painted the sky with the most vibrant sunset. For a moment we actually stopped and were stunned by your glory in creation.

Lord, please weave into our days moments that cause us to stand in awe of you. Help us to rejoice in the wonder of your ways. When we are engrossed in the minute details of life, help us to remind each other that every moment holds the potential to be a sacred God-moment. Increase our enjoyment of you when our hearts have become jaded and cynical. Thank you, God, for surprising us with your glory and splendor. Thank you for the ability to see how common people and experiences can actually prove to be quite glorious.

Everyone was gripped with great wonder and awe, and they praised God, exclaiming, "We have seen amazing things today!" LUKE 5:26

☼ A prayer about COMMITMENT
When your faithfulness changes me

HEAVENLY FATHER,

When I long to feel protected in the midst of change and unknowns, I love to dwell on your commitment to me. You keep your promises to watch over me and my family because we are yours. As I focus on your unchanging guard, I am changed. My faith is boosted, and my fears are soothed. Thank you for staying true to all the pledges you have made.

He will cover you with his feathers. He will shelter you with his wings. His faithful promises are your armor and protection. PSALM 91:4

☼ A prayer about MEMORIES
When I need to be intentional

LORD,

It seems only yesterday I brought this child home with me. It is so easy to get caught up in the day-to-day busyness that I forget to capture each moment. Help me to make positive memories for my child and me so that I don't let the days flit past without marking the stage my child is in right now. Help me to remember to stop and celebrate the small things.

Live wisely among those who are not believers, and make the most of every opportunity. COLOSSIANS 4:5

☼ A prayer about SERVICE
When I want to be served rather than serve

PRECIOUS LORD,

Snow brings the promise of a muddy floor. My children hurriedly track in evidence from the cold, damp world outside. As I mop the floor yet again, I admit that often my service to my family is not really about you. I am half-hearted in my efforts to help. My accomplishment in having a clean floor for a moment is not the only service you require of me.

Help me see that my work for my family and others can actually be an act of worship. In the simplest things, such as mopping, I can demonstrate to my children that my heart is wholly yours. You have given me breath and the ability to work as unto you. Remind me that as I serve them, I am actually serving you. Caring for the needs of my home is a privilege that some in this world do not have. Change my perspective today as I face the many known and unknown tasks that lie before me.

What does the LORD your God require of you? He requires only that you fear the LORD your God, and live in a way that pleases him, and love him and serve him with all your heart and soul. DEUTERONOMY 10:12

☼ A prayer about PARENTING
When I find joy in the journey

LORD,

Being a mother is one of the hardest things I have ever done, but it has been the most rewarding and joy-filled experience I have ever tackled. My child can be exasperating and exhausting one moment, but he can make me smile and laugh the next. The love I feel for this child goes beyond anything I could have imagined.

The thought that you love me exponentially more than I love my own child is incredible. Regardless of how many times I have let you down, you never give up on me. You love me unconditionally and extend grace to me more than I could ever earn or deserve. Thank you for being my loving Father and for showing me how to parent my own child through your example. Mold me to become more like you every day and to show my child unconditional love as you have shown me. Thank you for the gift of this precious life you have entrusted to me.

Whatever is good and perfect is a gift coming down to us from God our Father, who created all the lights in the heavens. He never changes or casts a shifting shadow.
JAMES 1:17

☼ **A prayer about LISTENING**
When I fail to hear you

LORD,

Sometimes I feel like I am talking to a wall! My teenager thinks she knows it all, and I watch helplessly as she makes poor choices. I wish she would just listen to me and the perspective I can bring to the situation. But don't I treat you exactly the same way? I stubbornly insist on forging my own path and ignore your quiet voice urging me to stop and listen to your wisdom. I think I know best and then still get surprised when I find I have made a poor decision.

Help me to stop and consult you when I'm faced with the big and small choices of life. Remind me that you have a perspective I do not have and you can help me avoid pain if I only listen to you and follow your guidance. Thank you for loving me despite my stubbornness. Guide my path today.

My child, listen to what I say, and treasure my commands. Tune your ears to wisdom, and concentrate on under-standing. Cry out for insight, and ask for understanding. Search for them as you would for silver; seek them like hidden treasures. Then you will understand what it means to fear the LORD, and you will gain knowledge of God.

PROVERBS 2:1-5

✦ A prayer about SPIRITUAL GIFTS
When I need to appreciate others' abilities

GOD,

Being in this family brings a wealth of blessings as well as a variety of challenges. You have divinely placed us together to shape us into your image. Each member of our family has different spiritual gifts, all necessary and complementary. But Lord, we need to better understand and appreciate each other's contributions. Please grant us patience and humility to learn how we can best work together in harmony.

I am thankful you have given my husband the gift of leadership. Where would we be without my son's gift of service to many others and to us? Continue to shape my daughter's heart for mercy and justice. I am grateful for opportunities to extend the gift of hospitality to our church family. Forgive us when we misunderstand each other and question motives. And please give us the privilege, Lord, of serving alongside one another for your glory.

God has given each of you a gift from his great variety of spiritual gifts. Use them well to serve one another.
I PETER 4:10

⚙ **A prayer about FATIGUE**
When we need new strength from you

FATHER,

Right now I wish my weary family and I could climb up into your arms and fall asleep hugged by you for a long, long time. Our home is worn out. I'm having trouble leading well because I'm at the end of my strength. You see us. You know. Long ago when you inspired Isaiah to write today's verses, you were seeing my children as they are now. Even they are worn out from the stress, the pace, the pressures.

Lord, increase our trust. Please begin with that gift so we can find new strength in you. Help us soar again on strong wings that are carried along by you. Help us run with renewed energy, and reinvigorate us to walk each step of our days full-hearted and fully recharged. I don't know how this will happen. I'm still tired. But I'm putting us at your mercy to show us how you will do these miracles in us. Thank you, Lord.

Even youths will become weak and tired, and young men will fall in exhaustion. But those who trust in the LORD will find new strength. They will soar high on wings like eagles. They will run and not grow weary. They will walk and not faint. ISAIAH 40:30-31

☼ **A prayer about ROLE MODELS**
When I desire consistency in my walk

LORD,

After a long week, I confess that rising early to spend time with you is a challenge. I know I desperately need this refueling to continue following you each day. I am always aware that little eyes are watching my habits too. Lord, I pray that I will provide a good spiritual example for my children to follow as they seek to walk with you.

Dear brothers and sisters, pattern your lives after mine, and learn from those who follow our example.
PHILIPPIANS 3:17

DAY 21 *Prayerful Moment*

☼ **A prayer about PATIENCE**
When I am frustrated

LORD,

With too many items on my to-do list today, I find myself becoming irritated and losing my composure way too easily. Help me tap into your Spirit and your unlimited supply of patience. I am unable to do it on my own.

May the Lord lead your hearts into a full understanding and expression of the love of God and the patient endurance that comes from Christ. 2 THESSALONIANS 3:5

DAY 22

☼ A prayer about DISCERNMENT
When I need clear vision about good versus best

JESUS,

Why is it so tempting for me to settle for less than the best? In a world that drives me to achieve, to be number one, to want more, more, more—I find myself grasping for a lot of what doesn't fully satisfy. Such is the human conundrum, I guess.

But Lord, I don't want to fall for those old tricks of the enemy that make something faulty appear glossy and worth coveting. Please give me discernment to see past the shallow view to the consequences of not heeding your Spirit's guidance for me and my family. Beyond merely helping me understand what's best, please give me your will to pursue those things, whether they involve relationships, material investments, spiritual focus, time management, or any other element of life. Expose my innermost thoughts and feelings.

And I ask you to grow my children's ability to discern your voice among all the others and give them a passion for your highest standards of love and godliness. Thank you for your gift of discernment that is life giving. May we not miss out on anything you have for us.

The word of God is alive and powerful. It is sharper than the sharpest two-edged sword. . . . It exposes our innermost thoughts and desires. HEBREWS 4:12

※ **A prayer about WORSHIP**
   When I need to acknowledge God's rule and reign

FATHER,

I praise you for you are worthy of praise. You are my King who sits on the throne. You sovereignly rule and reign over all of creation and its creatures. My only correct response is to bow before your holiness. I acknowledge that you are God, not me. You formed me and know the most intricate details about me. You chose me to be yours before the foundation of the earth was laid. Your ways are higher and deeper than I could ever comprehend.

May my friends and family see, in the choices I make, evidence of your supreme rule over my life. Forgive me for the times I try to seat myself upon the throne. Dethrone me and my self-centered agendas and plans. I am so thankful for the many ways your Word is a lamp to my feet and a light for my path. Your ways are right and perfect and demand my undying allegiance to you.

Come, let us worship and bow down. Let us kneel before the LORD our maker. PSALM 95:6

☼ **A prayer about TITHING**
   When I am tempted to doubt God's provision

LORD,

"Share fully, for all is the Lord's" is an attitude that my husband and I would like to live by. Even though we have sought to follow this over the years, I admit I am not as compelled to share as I used to be. I have gradually clenched my fists around all your gracious provisions to me. But what does it really matter if someone mistreats one of my possessions? They all belong to you anyway.

I commit to you, Lord, my desire to release my grasp on the things of this world. Develop a pattern in our home of bringing you an offering of the firstfruits of our labors. Increase our heart capacity to give to others. Remind my children and me that if we do not have what we perceive we need, in actuality we do not need it. You have promised that as we relinquish our hold on all you have given and as we dedicate it for your service, you will overwhelm us with the outpouring of your blessings.

"Bring all the tithes into the storehouse so there will be enough food in my Temple. If you do," says the LORD of Heaven's Armies, "I will open the windows of heaven for you. I will pour out a blessing so great you won't have enough room to take it in! Try it! Put me to the test!"
MALACHI 3:10

☼ A prayer about COMFORT
When I need to know you care

LORD,

Sometimes I feel drained by the neediness of others. Sympathy doesn't always come easily, especially when I feel as though I'm constantly picking someone up off the floor, emotionally. But then when it's my turn to feel weak, I wonder if I have the same effect on others. Do I drain you? No, I know your love is unlimited.

Thank you for the image in your Word of you bending down to listen to me. It shows me that you really do want to comfort me. Like most people, I crave compassion, and when I know you're not put off by my weaknesses, I'm drawn to love you more. Thank you for listening to me, for drawing near when I call to you. Knowing you want to help me makes such a difference in my hope and even in my ability to see myself strengthened again. Please grow my heart to offer that kind of acceptance and comfort to others when they hurt.

I love the LORD because he hears my voice and my prayer for mercy. Because he bends down to listen, I will pray as long as I have breath! PSALM 116:1-2

☼ A prayer about TESTING
When I fail the test of an undivided heart

ALMIGHTY GOD,

Time has flown, and we are now approaching the most challenging adventure yet—launching our children to college. These last few years have been filled with difficult academics and limitless extracurricular activities. Sometimes I wonder about the goal or aim we seem to have been pursuing. Is it strictly to achieve high test scores? Perhaps the culture is projecting the idea that a number or award defines true success. I fear this is a test we will fail every time.

As the constant pressure of measuring abilities and achievements surrounds us, may we be ever mindful that you do not value the external measurements as we do. You are intimately involved in a greater test, one that determines what captivates us. Examine our hearts for any wicked thoughts or intentions. Reveal where our hearts are divided and disloyal toward you. Forgive us for allowing areas in our lives to be paralyzed by anxiety and lack of trust. Thank you that even though we frequently fail the test of wholehearted faith, your love is unfailing.

Search me, O God, and know my heart; test me and know my anxious thoughts. PSALM 139:23

☼ A prayer about NEGLECT
When I ignore you

LORD,

I have been so busy with the challenges and demands of day-to-day life that I have not prioritized my relationship with you as I'd like. I long to spend time with you, O God, letting my roots sink deep into you, but I let other things get in the way. Forgive me for being absent. Usher me into your ever-loving presence today and fill my soul with your presence and peace.

I pray that God, the source of hope, will fill you completely with joy and peace because you trust in him.
ROMANS 15:13

DAY 28 *Prayerful Moment*

☼ A prayer about HUMILITY
When I think I know best

LORD,

Secretly I believe I know what's best for my child. It is easy to convince myself that my years of wisdom and life experience qualify me to feel this way. But deep down I know that this feeling is rooted in pride, which is not at all pleasing to you. Please remove all traces of pride in my parenting and replace it with humility and grateful dependence on you. Help me to seek your guidance rather than my own will.

He leads the humble in doing right, teaching them his way.
PSALM 25:9

☀ A prayer about MOTIVATION
When I need encouragement

FATHER,

Once again, I find myself struggling to find my own identity. I spend all my time caring for my child and my family, and I am getting lost. I am weary of the monotony of days spent changing diapers, cleaning a messy house, and trying to get my child to sleep. Each day seems to flow into the next. I can't help but wonder, am I accomplishing anything worthwhile, or am I slowly surrendering any chance to follow the dreams I once had? I am exhausted and don't see a light at the end of it all.

I need your reminder that you see all I am doing every day and that none of it is in vain. You have a plan for my life and for the talents and skills you have given me. Taking time to build into my family has worth and value beyond what I can see in this moment. Help me to remember that you want me to give my best to every task, no matter how small, and to trust that you will reward me some day for my efforts to live for you. Give me a spirit of gratefulness and thankfulness as I go about the mundane duties of my day. Help me to remember that I am a living demonstration of your love to my child.

Be strong and immovable. Always work enthusiastically for the Lord, for you know that nothing you do for the Lord is ever useless. I CORINTHIANS 15:58

☀ A prayer about LOVE
When I count my blessings

LORD,

When I look at this little child you have given me, I am completely overwhelmed with love in a way I have never experienced before. It has given me a whole new understanding of how much you love me. It makes me sad that I too often take your love for granted and don't give you the reverence you deserve. You are the almighty God, the maker of heaven and earth, and you call me your daughter.

Thank you for loving me and providing for me. Thank you for blessing me with this precious child. Help me to instill in my child a desire to follow you.

Dear friends, let us continue to love one another, for love comes from God. Anyone who loves is a child of God and knows God. But anyone who does not love does not know God, for God is love. God showed how much he loved us by sending his one and only Son into the world so that we might have eternal life through him. This is real love—not that we loved God, but that he loved us and sent his Son as a sacrifice to take away our sins. I JOHN 4:7-10

☀ A prayer about PERSEVERANCE
When I want to run away from pain

LORD,

When circumstances become hard or challenging, I some-times find myself fighting the urge to quit. When the going gets tough, I want to sit down and opt out rather than push through the struggles.

I believe that you will not give me more than I can handle in your strength, even though it feels like I can't handle this right now. Keep me open to the possibility that you may bring someone alongside me to help me shoul-der this load. Don't allow my pride to prevent me from accepting assistance. In the meantime, help me to push through and persevere despite my fatigue. Remind me of your promise to be with me. Give me the courage and the strength to endure. Be my rock and my refuge when life is hard. Thank you for giving me all that I need to get through today.

Dear brothers and sisters, when troubles of any kind come your way, consider it an opportunity for great joy. For you know that when your faith is tested, your endurance has a chance to grow. JAMES 1:2-3

☀ A prayer about WORRY
When I am filled with anxiety

GOD,

You know how often I feel trapped by my past sins. This obsession can cause me to doubt your love and forgiveness. And fear about my future and my potential fruitfulness can drive me to despair.

O Lord, please replace my doubts with confidence. I want to be convinced deep in my soul that absolutely nothing in the past or the future will ever be able to separate me from your love. When I consider my past, help me remember that Jesus' blood on the cross is sufficient to atone for any sin. When I consider my present, show me that anxiety is an occasion to move swiftly to you in prayer. When I fret over my future, remind me that you hold it firmly within your grasp. Replace my fears with an emboldened faith.

I am convinced that nothing can ever separate us from God's love. Neither death nor life, neither angels nor demons, neither our fears for today nor our worries about tomorrow—not even the powers of hell can separate us from God's love.
ROMANS 8:38

☀ **A prayer about PATIENCE**
   When I just want to rest

LORD,

The middle of the night is not my best time. When I hear my baby's demanding cries, I feel so tired and frustrated. I don't want to crawl out of my warm bed to attend to someone else's needs. I find myself losing patience and getting angry. I know that this time is precious and soon I will long for the alone time with my little one, snuggling in the rocking chair, but today I just want peace and quiet.

Help me to slow down and get the proper perspective. Remind me that this will pass, and all too soon my child will be grown. Give me the patience to deal with the lack of sleep, and help me not to take out my frustration on my innocent child. Flood me with your love.

Always be humble and gentle. Be patient with each other, making allowance for each other's faults because of your love. Make every effort to keep yourselves united in the Spirit, binding yourselves together with peace.

EPHESIANS 4:2-3

✴ **A prayer about WORRY**
   When I am burdened down with cares

MY SAVIOR,

My mind is racing as I consider my situation from all angles. I'm not sure where to turn for answers, so I look to you for wisdom. I surrender my desire to control this situation. Your Word encourages me to trust in your perfect plan for my life. Give me the grace to exchange my problems for your peace.

Worry weighs a person down; an encouraging word cheers a person up. PROVERBS 12:25

DAY 35 *Prayerful Moment*

✴ **A prayer about CARING**
   When I want to encourage active consideration

LORD,

Please help my children understand that caring involves action. Sometimes action means prayer and prayer alone. But true caring often requires entering into someone's trouble, listening attentively, offering help even when it's inconvenient, and working to see a situation from someone else's viewpoint. Please help me to show my family how to care through the way I care for them and others around me.

Share each other's burdens, and in this way obey the law of Christ. GALATIANS 6:2

☼ A prayer about HABITS
When I am embarrassed about my behavior

LORD,

I am so convicted when I see my children pick up my bad habits. No matter what the bad habit is and how cute they seem when they are doing it, it is an ugly reminder of my own sin. I don't want to pass along negative habits to my children. I want them to be reflections of the fruit of your Spirit.

Help me to focus my thoughts on you so that others can see your reflection in me. Shine through me so they can learn how to be patient and kind, gentle and self-controlled. You are the ultimate example for both me and my children. Thank you for guiding our path. Help me to give over my sinful habits to you so you can mold me and shape me into your likeness.

Since you have heard about Jesus and have learned the truth that comes from him, throw off your old sinful nature and your former way of life, which is corrupted by lust and deception. Instead, let the Spirit renew your thoughts and attitudes. Put on your new nature, created to be like God— truly righteous and holy. EPHESIANS 4:21-24

❋ A prayer about BURNOUT
When I see my children pushing too hard

JESUS,

Lately I've been watching my kids fall further into the trap of our striving society. What began as healthy determination has gradually been warped into pressure to perform at all costs. Balance, inner well-being, spiritual focus, family time, rest—all have fallen victim to the lie that we must work ourselves to the bone to be successful.

Lord, my kids are worth so much more than this consuming lifestyle. Please show them that their worth, their success, is not defined by how much they strive. In fact, if their efforts are not backed by you, then burnout is inevitable. Please show them balance. Slow them down if necessary, but please help them learn easily so they won't need a major jolt to get them to see their need for your rest. None of us can push 24/7; you didn't design us for that. Thank you for valuing downtime and for setting such a great example of taking time out for what's most important.

Unless the LORD builds a house, the work of the builders is wasted. . . . It is useless for you to work so hard from early morning until late at night, anxiously working for food to eat; for God gives rest to his loved ones. PSALM 127:1-2

☀ A prayer about JUDGING OTHERS
When I need a reminder of how God sees them

LORD JESUS,

I learn a lot from watching the children around me. It is so easy for them to tattle and blame. They want a parent to step in and make the other person do what they want them to do.

How often do I do the same thing? I see others acting in a way I think deserves correction or a reprimand. I want you to come down and set them straight. Remind me that it is not my job to judge the behavior of others. Help me to focus only on my own behavior and thoughts as I go about my day. Show me how to love others in a way that will draw them to you.

She came to Jesus and said, "Lord, doesn't it seem unfair to you that my sister just sits here while I do all the work? Tell her to come and help me." But the Lord said to her, "My dear Martha, you are worried and upset over all these details! There is only one thing worth being concerned about. Mary has discovered it, and it will not be taken away from her." LUKE 10:40-42

☸ A prayer about INFLUENCES
When I am filling my mind with garbage

JESUS,

Each and every day I am assaulted with negative images. Whether it is the violent scenes I watch on television, the constant clamor for more that I hear in commercials, or the scantily clad bodies I see on the magazine covers at the supermarket, these pictures and appeals are all vying for my attention. Yet they are not always filled with content that is pleasing to you.

It is easy to get sucked into the latest gossip or television program that everyone else seems to be talking about. I don't want to feel left out. But I know that your desire for me is to keep my mind and heart pure. One way to do that is to monitor the things I watch. Help me to realize when I should walk away or turn off some of the images of the world that might be damaging to my soul. In doing so, may I model discernment and self-control to my children. Fill my mind with the thoughts that you want to use to mold me and shape me. Help me to dwell on those instead of worldly things.

Fix your thoughts on what is true, and honorable, and right, and pure, and lovely, and admirable. Think about things that are excellent and worthy of praise.

PHILIPPIANS 4:8

☼ A prayer about NEEDS
When I feel overwhelmed by demands

LORD,

This little one you have entrusted to me has so many needs and is not afraid to demand that I meet them immediately. I am only one person and I can't be everything for this child, no matter how much I love him. I am stretching myself so thin trying to do it all that I feel myself breaking. I lose my temper or find myself on the edge of tears way too easily. I need to stop and step back for some perspective.

Help me to evaluate which things I need to do and which things I can let go. Remind me that I don't need to accomplish everything on my own, but that it is all right to ask others for help. Renew my energy and give me the strength to carry on. Bring people into my life to help bear the load during this stressful time. And most of all, give me hope that this too will pass and that there are brighter days ahead. Carry me through until that time comes.

I love the LORD because he hears my voice and my prayer for mercy. Because he bends down to listen, I will pray as long as I have breath! PSALM 116:1-2

☼ A prayer about RESPONSIBILITY
  When I forget who my brother is

GOD,

I saw so many familiar faces today—as I worked out at the gym, as I walked out to my mailbox, as I shopped at the grocery store. I'm not sure, however, how many people I actually noticed. Soften my heart with your compassion to love those who cross my path. They are my brothers and sisters, and I am called to give your Good News to them.

Afterward the LORD asked Cain, "Where is your brother? Where is Abel?" "I don't know," Cain responded. "Am I my brother's guardian?" GENESIS 4:9

DAY 42 *Prayerful Moment*

☼ A prayer about the HOLY SPIRIT
  When I need wisdom

LORD,

I don't know what to do or how to handle this situation. It is beyond my human capabilities. I need your Spirit to guide my steps today. Thank you for providing me with your wisdom, which far surpasses my understanding.

We do not use words that come from human wisdom. Instead, we speak words given to us by the Spirit, using the Spirit's words to explain spiritual truths.
I CORINTHIANS 2:13

☀ A prayer about STUBBORNNESS
When I need a soft and compliant heart

FATHER,

My daughter is sometimes overconfident and can be very independent. From an early age she always wanted to do things all on her own. Because of my *own* stubborn tendencies, we have at times experienced conflict over this mutual struggle. Lord, please help me to model for her a steady dependence on you. Your Word says that as I rely on you, life inevitably runs more smoothly.

Help me forsake my prideful overconfidence in my gifts. Incline me to listen to you rather than place my trust in my self-sufficient plans. I admit that I will never be up to the task of orchestrating and controlling my life or my daughter's life. Keep us moving forward rather than backward. Give both of us occasions that serve to open our eyes to our desperate need for your intervention. I have no doubt that in love, you will bring us to the end of our individual resources rather quickly. Please make our hearts compliant. Empower us with your strength to yield to your call and be quick to obey.

But my people would not listen to me. They kept doing whatever they wanted, following the stubborn desires of their evil hearts. They went backward instead of forward.
JEREMIAH 7:24

☼ A prayer about STRESS
When I am captured by tension

FATHER,

I feel so weighed down by life. As the day progresses, instead of relinquishing my cares, I allow them to pile one upon the other. Over time these burdens feel as though they will crush me. These worries disorient and confuse me. Where should I turn? How will I cope? Who holds my future? All these questions muddy my thinking and leave me feeling overwhelmed. I am not sure I will be able to carry these concerns another day.

Forgive me, Father, for my independent and self-reliant ways. I often live as though I actually think I can control my world and solve all my problems. I surrender my troubles and lay them at your feet. I acknowledge that you and you alone have the wisdom and power to address my concerns. Help me to rest securely in your providential plan. Help me to fight the tendency to live in bondage to my fears.

Give all your worries and cares to God, for he cares about you. I PETER 5:7

DAY 45

☸ A prayer about WORDS
When my speech fails to please God

SPIRIT,

I confess that yesterday as we sat in our small group, I answered questions with the intent of trying to impress others. I felt insecure about being a stay-at-home mother, and I wanted others to value my contributions. But you, Lord, also heard those prideful words. I desperately want the words of my mouth to please you.

Help me live and speak in such a way that demonstrates to the world that I have an audience of One. Conform my thoughts and reflections to your Word so that they will delight you. When I am tempted to place my security in other people's approval of me, please remind me that your view of me is all that matters. You are my solid ground and my Helper. Fill my mouth with your praise. Guard my lips to say only what reflects worship and honor of you.

May the words of my mouth and the meditation of my heart be pleasing to you, O LORD, my rock and my redeemer.
PSALM 19:14

❀ A prayer about DISAPPOINTMENT
When I need to show my child true hope

LORD,

I saw it on her face again: disappointment at another of life's blows. Even during a fairly good year, she'll face disappointment now and then. This has been a particularly tough few months. I can't blame her for feeling negative more and more lately, and my heart hurts for her.

Father, I want to show her what it means to put her deepest hope in you, because when our hearts are aligned with what you want for us, you reveal to us that things will still turn out okay—better even. But right now life hurts her, God. Please help me balance understanding her pain with modeling what it means to firmly hope in your goodness and overcoming power. Tenaciously putting her hope in you will reveal so much more to her than she can see now.

You have beautiful plans for her, Lord. I praise you for that and trust that her hope in you will not disappoint, regardless of current circumstances.

Endurance develops strength of character, and character strengthens our confident hope of salvation. And this hope will not lead to disappointment. For we know how dearly God loves us, because he has given us the Holy Spirit to fill our hearts with his love. ROMANS 5:4-5

☼ A prayer about INVOLVEMENT
When I need community

MY FATHER,

Raising a family can be exhausting, and sometimes the thought of rallying everyone together and getting out the door to church can be overwhelming. I am tempted to skip it and rest. But your Word encourages me to make an effort to be in fellowship with other believers.

You remind me that coming together for corporate worship and teaching nourishes my soul and helps me and my family to grow. You remind me that iron sharpens iron and that being with other believers brings accountability into my life. I am spurred on toward deeper relationships by being with others. You also remind me that I can give back to the church, even in this parenting season, by volunteering, giving my tithe, or even just smiling and making others feel welcome. I am so grateful for the opportunity to worship you each week in the company of others who know you.

Let us think of ways to motivate one another to acts of love and good works. And let us not neglect our meeting together, as some people do, but encourage one another, especially now that the day of his return is drawing near.
HEBREWS 10:24-25

☼ A prayer about EXAMPLE
When my words seem to fall on deaf ears

LORD,

If a picture says a thousand words, help me to be a picture of your character for my children to observe. Too many words from me leaves them either glassy-eyed or angry, so close my mouth when necessary and instead help me live as an example of your holiness. Even when their ears are closed, may their eyes be open to notice you in me.

In the same way, let your good deeds shine out for all to see, so that everyone will praise your heavenly Father.
MATTHEW 5:16

DAY 49 *Prayerful Moment*

☼ A prayer about REST
When I need a Sabbath

GOD,

Reading about the Sabbath reminds me that you rested after creating the world and that one day you will lead me to my final rest. I confess to you my addiction to my well-worn rhythms, which make quiet and calm hard to come by during the week. God, on this day you've set aside for me to rest, I ask you to help me to still my body, mind, and spirit as you refresh and restore my soul.

And God blessed the seventh day and declared it holy, because it was the day when he rested from all his work of creation.
GENESIS 2:3

⚜ **A prayer about LETTING GO**
  When I need help remembering the goal

GRACIOUS FATHER,

The hardest thing about raising kids is realizing that I will someday need to let them go out into the world all by themselves. I find myself wanting to grab them and hold on tight. I want to protect them from the realities of life and shelter them from anything bad that might happen.

I need help remembering that ultimately my children belong to you. You have promised to be with them always, and I need to trust that you will work all of the things that happen to them, both positive and negative, together for their good and their growth. Help me to teach my children to be independent, giving them more freedom as they grow so that they will be prepared to go out into the world. Protect my heart as I watch them make mistakes and fall down. Be with them and take root in their hearts so they can withstand the pressures of life. But most of all, give me strength to let them go when the time comes.

Do not be afraid or discouraged, for the LORD will personally go ahead of you. He will be with you; he will neither fail you nor abandon you. DEUTERONOMY 31:8

☼ A prayer about DETERMINATION
When my kids need long-range focus

LORD,

I love it when my children discover something important to them. Keep them passionate about the most meaningful ventures of life. Show me how to nurture seeds of passion for your pursuits so that everything else they love spending time on grows from their first love of you. Help them seek to recognize your voice, and then keep them following you as they grow. They will need true, long-lasting determination to continue living for your prize in a world that will try hard to pull them away from you.

Let them know they are in a race that will last throughout life. Free them from competing against anyone else, but instead help them to stay true to you. If they steer off onto a dangerous path, in your grace trip them up. Let their wounds be the small ones of your discipline that will help them avoid more painful ones of sin and regret. Burn into their hearts the vision of themselves as winners of your rewards, and let that vision keep them determinedly on course toward your heart.

Don't you realize that in a race everyone runs, but only one person gets the prize? So run to win!
I CORINTHIANS 9:24

✷ A prayer about SIGNIFICANCE
When I deem the wrong things worthy

HEAVENLY FATHER,

I admit that I can be easily impressed by the accomplishments of others and can quickly put them on pedestals. Sometimes this tendency even changes the way I relate to them. You have convicted me about this issue—that I rarely esteem the things that you appreciate. I tend to focus more on the externals, while you look at what is on the inside of a person.

Forgive me, Lord, for showing preferential regard to others. And cleanse me from comparing myself to others. In your economy, the first will be last and the last will be first. I acknowledge that I do not always appreciate or understand your perspective. God, I surrender my need to feel as though I can really understand your will. I long to see others the way you do. Point out areas where I am blind to the things that you find worthy and valuable. Help me to value others and acknowledge their significance.

Many who are the greatest now will be least important then, and those who seem least important now will be the greatest then. MATTHEW 19:30

DAY 53

☸ A prayer about HOLINESS
When I need inspiration

LORD,

As my child grows, I want to give him the tools he needs to navigate the world around him. I want him to learn to live a life of holiness, set apart from the world. I want him to learn to look to you for guidance, not to the media or his peers. But holiness has gotten a bad rap in society, and its definition has been twisted.

Help me to show him that holiness is not about a list of rules to follow. Holiness is rooted in a relationship with you and a desire to please you with thoughts and deeds. You have not asked him to be perfect. You have sent your Son to earth to die for our sins. You look at the heart. There is no way anyone can ever reach perfect holiness because no one is holy like you are. But we can look to you to guide our steps each day and help us walk in your ways. Help me teach my son to learn to be more like you every day.

Hannah prayed: "My heart rejoices in the LORD! The LORD has made me strong. Now I have an answer for my enemies; I rejoice because you rescued me. No one is holy like the LORD! There is no one besides you; there is no Rock like our God." I SAMUEL 2:1-2

☀ **A prayer about SAFETY**
When I need to rest in God's protection

SOVEREIGN LORD,

We have just returned safely from travel across the country. Often I take your providential care of my family and me for granted. Thank you for keeping us safe and for the opportunities to interact with many different cultures and surroundings. I confess, God, that when I am out of my familiar paths, I can feel a little insecure. Being out of control in any environment tends to bring fear and uncertainty to my heart.

When my children were born, I declared that they belonged to you. I was confident in those moments that their protection and provision were firmly in your grip. Yet as the years have gone by, I have slipped into actually thinking I can ensure their protection and safety. Forgive me, Lord, for seeking to try to coordinate circumstances that are beyond my control. I am comforted and encouraged that in some of your last moments on earth you had our well-being and care in the forefront of your mind and heart.

I'm not asking you to take them out of the world, but to keep them safe from the evil one. JOHN 17:15

☼ A prayer about DISTRACTIONS
When I need you to focus me

LORD,

In this world full of interests that distract me from you, let your presence keep me so amazed that nothing comes between us. Let your Word be my constant, heavenly distraction from all that entices me to what isn't of you. Please help my children learn to focus on you as well, so that they may enjoy years without regret, filled with your Spirit.

Oh, how I love your instructions! I think about them all day long. PSALM 119:97

DAY 56 *Prayerful Moment*

☼ A prayer about ENCOURAGEMENT
When I would love to feel your smile on me

LORD,

Some days it seems no matter how I try, someone is griping about what I'm doing wrong or not doing exactly the way they'd like. You must feel griped at so much more than I feel it. How about if we encourage each other today, Lord? I praise you for being so good and holy and kind. And would you please smile on me today simply because I'm yours?

It has pleased the LORD to make you his very own people.
I SAMUEL 12:22

☀ A prayer about FRUSTRATION
When I feel that I can't go on

HEAVENLY FATHER,

It's been one of those days. My schedule was disrupted around breakfast time, and things never got back on track. I need you to renew my strength and remind me of why I am here. Show me how all of my effort and struggle are shaping and molding not only my children, but me as well, into reflections of you. You love me and care for me and have me exactly where you want me.

Thank you for entrusting these children to my care. Help me to be an accurate reflection of your unrelenting love in their lives. And may they learn from me how to look to you for the help and hope only a loving Father can provide.

We can rejoice, too, when we run into problems and trials, for we know that they help us develop endurance. And endurance develops strength of character, and character strengthens our confident hope of salvation. And this hope will not lead to disappointment. For we know how dearly God loves us, because he has given us the Holy Spirit to fill our hearts with his love. ROMANS 5:3-5

☼ A prayer about ADOPTION
When I see so many children at risk

FATHER,

I can't help but pause with that one word. I didn't come up with that name for you; you call yourself my heavenly Father. I cherish what your identification with that name means to me. You designed fatherhood as such a powerful role. Yet how many children do not know what it means to live with the security of an earthly father's love, guidance, and protection—much less to be held by your perfect care?

You long to adopt each of us as your child, but so many young ones around the globe literally are dying inside and out to be cherished, to belong, to identify with a loving family. Will you be "father to the fatherless" today, as you promise in Psalm 68:5? Overflow the heart of each one who needs your fatherly care. Rescue, heal, and rebuild lives that have been destroyed by the absence of love. And show me how I can adopt a more active role in loving a needy child as well.

Pure and genuine religion in the sight of God the Father means caring for orphans and widows in their distress and refusing to let the world corrupt you. JAMES 1:27

☼ A prayer about REJECTION
When I feel left out

LORD,

The hurt and disappointment of once again being left out is so painful to our son. He longs to be included and embraced by the group. Help me, Lord, to encourage him to continue to persevere in building relationships with others. When I see that hurt look in his eyes, I can relate to the feelings of loneliness and isolation. I often wonder if anyone can understand how we feel.

Thank you, Lord, that you are our Savior who was despised and rejected. You were treated as an outcast, even turned away by many who at one time had followed you. Being an outsider is something that you understand and to which you willingly subjected yourself for our sakes. You were set outside the gates to suffer and die in our place so that we could be insiders in your family. Lord, you have blessed us, even in this struggle, to share in the fellowship of your sufferings.

Jesus suffered and died outside the city gates to make his people holy by means of his own blood. HEBREWS 13:12

☀ A prayer about ATTITUDE
When I need you to overhaul mine

JESUS,

I'm battling a rotten attitude these days. My griping heart is not blessing anyone. I miss having your attitude of love and gracious truth, so I surely need you to overhaul mine. It's beyond fixing on my own. I'm not even sure why my thoughts tend to run downhill. I could blame it on world events, uncertainty in life's circumstances, days that aren't going well. Feeling stuck in my shortcomings is driving me batty. My attitude struggles hinder the fullness of your Spirit shining through me.

But Lord, you promise strength for all situations. I love that this verse begins with "But." It shows that you know I can't grow spiritual fruit without your help. Please bathe me with your truth, your hope, your patience, mercy, and gratitude. Transform the "less" of my mind and heart with the "more" of yourself. Clear away the weeds so the produce of your Spirit can thrive. Only by your power can I have an attitude like yours (Philippians 2:5). Thank you for not letting me feel content until you work into me the growth I need. Please help me be teachable so I'll bless you and those you care about.

But the Holy Spirit produces this kind of fruit in our lives: love, joy, peace, patience, kindness, goodness, faithfulness, gentleness, and self-control. GALATIANS 5:22-23

☀ A prayer about FOLLOWING GOD
When I want to model your love

LORD,

My deepest desire is to see my children grow up and follow you wholeheartedly. I know that I can help build this foundation in their lives by modeling for them my relationship with you. Enable me to make our home a loving, Christ-filled place where they can learn about you. Help me instill in them good values and morals. Make our home a refuge from the world, but not a place to hide from the world.

Even now, open up opportunities for our family to serve together in our neighborhood, community, or church so that my children may experience the joy that comes from helping others and honoring you. Show me how to create a balance for them so they can stand strong in their convictions without fear when they go out into the world as adults.

Anyone who listens to my teaching and follows it is wise, like a person who builds a house on solid rock. Though the rain comes in torrents and the floodwaters rise and the winds beat against that house, it won't collapse because it is built on bedrock. MATTHEW 7:24-25

☼ **A prayer about TENDERNESS**
When I need to extend gentle and patient care

LORD,

Why do I withhold tender words and actions toward my children? Perhaps the cause is my constant battle with impatience. Maybe I act that way because I don't feel they deserve such consideration because of their behavior. Lord, you never withhold your compassionate mercies from me. Your unfailing love serves as a hedge of protection. Make me a conduit of your tenderness to my children today.

LORD, don't hold back your tender mercies from me. Let your unfailing love and faithfulness always protect me.
PSALM 40:11

☼ **A prayer about THANKFULNESS**
When I have something great to share

LORD,

Good news has a tendency to travel fast. Sharing a picture of a happy family event, for instance, takes only a moment. So why has so much time elapsed since I shared with others how thankful I am for you in my life? Cultivate in me an excitement to shout your greatness from the mountaintops. May everyone I encounter hear the praise of your incomparable greatness on my lips.

Give thanks to the LORD and proclaim his greatness. Let the whole world know what he has done. PSALM 105:1

☼ A prayer about CHILDREN
When I need to entrust them to you

GOD,

People warned me that having children would show me a kind of love I'd never felt. Their words were quite the understatement. I can't imagine another way to lay my heart bare quite like loving my child. Split me open, pour me out. Can there be any greater vulnerability than loving the vulnerable, any fiercer heartache than feeling theirs along with them?

Nothing strikes fear in me more than my children facing danger or illness or an accident I can't prevent or fix. What do I do with all of it, God? Sometimes the intensity of this motherly love feels overwhelming. Lord, when uncertainty and fear for my kids war within me, please overflow me with peace that only you can offer—peace that leads me to rest, knowing that they are your children first. You promise to teach them and lead them to your peace as well. Please give them hearts for you and a willingness to be led by you. Guard them and guide them in ways I can't. Help them search relentlessly for your face and bathe them in peace. Me too, Lord.

I will teach all your children, and they will enjoy great peace. ISAIAH 54:13

❀ A prayer about CHOICES
When my kids need to learn the power of their decisions

LORD,

If we could have the wisdom of age when we're young, how might we do things differently in those early years? I watch my growing kids and wonder how much they think about the random decisions they make throughout each day. Sometimes I worry when it seems like they're preoccupied by foolish pastimes. Youth can be so full of fun, but it also includes a sea of temptations that can pull their immature hearts in directions they'll regret.

Father, I don't want my kids to live their lives weighed down by regrets of foolish choices they made when they were young. Please impress on them the value of paying attention to your instruction, of respecting the rules that I set for their good. Please don't let them become so sure of themselves that they think they've got all the answers. And help me to steer them without causing them extra frustrations. Thanks for leading me as I do my best to lead them.

My child, never forget the things I have taught you. Store my commands in your heart. If you do this, you will live many years, and your life will be satisfying. . . . Trust in the LORD with all your heart; do not depend on your own understanding. PROVERBS 3:1-2, 5

☼ A prayer about SELF-ESTEEM
When I need to remember the origin of our worth

GOD,

I have heard the message one too many times that in order to have healthy children, we need to boost their self-esteem. God, as much as I love and cherish my children, my affection is always secondary to your primary love for them. You love and treasure them far more than I ever could. Your Word tells them that this love is incapable of failing and is everlasting.

God, I am thankful that you treat all of us as your beloved children. I am grateful that you even know the number of hairs on each of our heads. How could I rest at night if I did not believe that you had a loving and gracious plan for all of our lives? You go before us, lighting the path so that we can follow you. We have worth only because of you, Lord, and we esteem and honor you for the compassion and care you freely give to each of us.

Long ago the LORD said to Israel: "I have loved you, my people, with an everlasting love. With unfailing love I have drawn you to myself." JEREMIAH 31:3

☀ A prayer about LIMITATIONS
When I want to fix my child's problems

LORD,

When something goes wrong for my child, how I wish I could always provide a solution. I get so frustrated when I want to make it better and there is nothing I can do. When my child is sick, I want to be able to heal her immediately. When my child is feeling lonely, I want to ensure that everyone includes her. When she is struggling with depression, I want to make her happy. But I am only human, and there is only so much I can do.

How comforting it is to know that you are God, and that you can heal and comfort and give your peace that passes understanding. While I may not be able to fix my child's hurt, you can. You love my child even more than I can imagine. You know what she needs even more than I do. You can see how this situation is growing her and preparing her for the future. Please be there for her today in all the ways that I can't. I choose to give my frustration and worry over to you.

You will keep in perfect peace all who trust in you, all whose thoughts are fixed on you! Trust in the LORD always, for the LORD GOD is the eternal Rock. . . . LORD, you will grant us peace; all we have accomplished is really from you.
ISAIAH 26:3-4, 12

❀ **A prayer about SUFFERING**
When I must be still and endure pain

GOD,

This unexpected injury has sidelined me, and I have to discard my well-intentioned plans and agendas. The pain is ever-present and continually distracts me from focusing on daily life. I am so frustrated that I cannot do what I had planned, and my to-do list is growing longer. I wonder how the needs of my family will be taken care of. All I can do is lie here and be still.

Perhaps that is exactly where you want me to be at this season of my life, totally dependent on you. Give me patience and teach me what it means to be a gracious receiver of help from others. I am thankful for their care and anticipate the day when I can come alongside others to care for them. Since you have ordained this suffering, would you show me how to steward my experience as I begin recovery? Thank you for your constant comfort and care. I sense your presence in the stillness of my life. Give me opportunities to reciprocate the comfort I have so generously received from others. And please help me grow a contentment and thankfulness that will overflow during these difficult days.

We are confident that as you share in our sufferings,
you will also share in the comfort God gives us.
2 CORINTHIANS 1:7

☼ **A prayer about WORDS**
   When I want my mouth to speak life-giving truth

PRECIOUS LORD,

I enjoy expressing my creativity by trying new recipes. My
day is made whenever my kids or husband compliment me
on a meal (or even ask for seconds!). Remind me that wise
words can have the same satisfying impact as any comfort
food. They please you and nourish my family. Speaking the
right truth in love at the right time glorifies you. Keep this
reality ever before my thoughts and words.

*Wise words satisfy like a good meal; the right words bring
satisfaction.* PROVERBS 18:20

DAY 70 *Prayerful Moment*

☼ **A prayer about SALVATION**
   When I am grateful to God for the gift of Jesus

HEAVENLY FATHER,

Thank you for sending your Son to earth especially for me.
I am overwhelmed with gratitude for your grace, and I long
to share this gift with my children. Could you help me not
to overlook any opportunity to pass on the Good News of
your Son to my kids today?

*There is only one God and one Mediator who can reconcile
God and humanity—the man Christ Jesus. He gave his life
to purchase freedom for everyone.* I TIMOTHY 2:5-6

☀ A prayer about RECONCILIATION
When I want to be right

GOD,

As I lie here staring at the ceiling, surrounded by darkness and tears, help me, dear God. I know I am right, or at least I think I am. If only my husband would understand and see things from my perspective. I know I was a little bit cruel to him with my words today, but I can't help but feel that if I had spoken just a bit louder or stronger, he would finally have appreciated my viewpoint.

God, I am not sure how we are going to move back toward one another. Right now my heart is hard and cold; I do not want to seek reconciliation. Yet I know this is not how it should be. You have forgiven so much in my life; how can I knowingly withhold forgiveness from my dear husband? Break my heart, O God. Help me to be quick to repent in all my relationships, especially my marriage. Forgive me, Lord, for lying here one second more than I should. Help me move closer to you; then I know I will move closer to him.

Be kind to each other, tenderhearted, forgiving one another, just as God through Christ has forgiven you.
EPHESIANS 4:32

☼ A prayer about SORROW
When I feel overwhelmed by a broken heart

PRECIOUS SAVIOR,

I ache over the loss of a child that I never got to hold. Many nights I cry myself to sleep, wondering when the pain will subside. Even though I know every child belongs to you, I am finding difficulty in comprehending my empty nursery. My heart is heavy with the burden of a child who was never brought home.

Help me remember that my grief is but for a night and that joy will come in the morning to my sad soul. Jesus, give me endurance to love and care for my family during this ongoing struggle. I remember your assurance that one day we will experience no more tears or sorrow. I look forward to that day with ever-increasing expectancy. You have promised to wipe away my tears and heal my broken heart. I offer my broken spirit to you. You alone can make it whole again.

He will wipe every tear from their eyes, and there will be no more death or sorrow or crying or pain. All these things are gone forever. REVELATION 21:4

☼ A prayer about FAILURE
When it bares its teeth at me

JESUS,

The bite of failure is tearing hard today. From the minute I woke up, I've been feeling inadequate, kicking myself for not being enough in this daily life. My ideal self is not always gracious to my real self; my ideal self believes I should have a better track record for following through, for living creatively and graciously, for bringing style and class and productivity to everything I attempt. My ideal self notes that if I were more together, I wouldn't waste time feeling not good enough!

Lord, please remove the blinders from my ideal self and refocus her according to the way you see me. I am not a failure in your eyes, and for that I'm so grateful. Thank you for the security you offer when I don't feel good enough. Please speak wholeness to my soul today. I can do all things through you because you give me your strength, and how ideal is that?

Each time he said, "My grace is all you need. My power works best in weakness." So now I am glad to boast about my weaknesses, so that the power of Christ can work through me. . . . For when I am weak, then I am strong.

2 CORINTHIANS 12:9-10

☼ A prayer about DECISIONS
When the answer isn't clear

GOD,

More often than ever these days, I struggle to know what decisions are best for my kids. Things seemed easier when they were tiny: nap or no nap, cereal at four months or six, preschool at age three or four? I weighed each one as vital back then, but now those choices seem pretty simple and obvious compared to the pressures of these later years.

How do I balance social freedoms with boundaries? How can I help my children claim their identity in you? What do I say (or not say) when I don't care for their choice of a friend or dating relationship? And why do I sweat these things so long before remembering that you offer your guidance to those who seek your presence? I can have these shadows of doubt lifted if I'll bathe myself in the light of your Word. Lord, please help me to seek you above all else so that I can offer my children the best direction you have to offer. And please help them learn to seek you first as well.

Your word is a lamp to guide my feet and a light for my path.
PSALM 119:105

☀ A prayer about being OVERWHELMED
When I am carrying too much

LORD,

My schedule is full to overflowing. I have so many pressures and expectations vying for my time and attention. I am not sure how I am supposed to get through them all. I am afraid I am going to drop the ball and let everyone down, including myself. You have asked me to give you my burdens and my cares, and yet here I am again, trying to do it all in my own strength.

Help me stop and take a breath so that I may give over all of my stress to you. Help me see how you can lift the weight of my day and show me the way to find rest in the midst of it all. Thank you for lifting my problems onto your shoulders so I don't have to carry them alone. Give me your strength to get through the day.

Jesus said, "Come to me, all of you who are weary and carry heavy burdens, and I will give you rest. Take my yoke upon you. Let me teach you, because I am humble and gentle at heart, and you will find rest for your souls. For my yoke is easy to bear, and the burden I give you is light."
MATTHEW 11:28-30

☀ **A prayer about WITNESSING**
   When I want truth rather than opinions

FATHER,

For years I have gathered with the same mothers as our children play. Sometimes our conversation is superficial. But other times we talk about weightier matters. Help me to know when to sprinkle the truth of the gospel into our conversations. Guide my words so they encourage my friends when they're discouraged. I pray these women will understand that I am basing my life and faith on *truth*, not on worldly wisdom or my own opinions.

Dear brothers and sisters, I want you to understand that the gospel message I preach is not based on mere human reasoning.
GALATIANS 1:11

DAY 77 *Prayerful Moment*

☀ **A prayer about the POWER OF GOD**
   When I need to rest in a power greater than my own

GOD,

I am so tired of trying—trying to do things in my own strength, trying to overcome what seem to be immovable obstacles, trying to reconcile broken relationships. I am so tired of trying to be you. Help me to relinquish my dependence on self-sufficiency and rest in the truth that with you all things are possible.

Jesus looked at them intently and said, "Humanly speaking, it is impossible. But with God everything is possible."
MATTHEW 19:26

☼ A prayer about WORRY
When I fret over God's provision for my family

LORD ABOVE,

I am sitting here at my desk wondering if we will have enough money at the end of the month. Our expenses seem to have increased exponentially this year; yet, unfortunately, our income has not kept pace with our financial responsibilities. I know that life is more than just material goods, but I find myself consumed by acquiring what I deem to be enough. I know instinctively that I will never have enough to feel satisfied, but voicing my anxieties will not add any resources to my account or time to my calendar.

You are the maker and maintainer of all things. I surrender my need to try to control my circumstances and their outcomes. You have always provided not only for my family's needs but also for many of our wants, and I know that you firmly hold our future. Now please align my thoughts to this truth so that I might walk in your peace.

That is why I tell you not to worry about everyday life—whether you have enough food and drink, or enough clothes to wear. Isn't life more than food, and your body more than clothing? MATTHEW 6:25

☼ A prayer about COMPROMISE
When I don't want to meet halfway

LORD,

I don't want to compromise this time. I'm sick of feeling like I'm missing half of myself by compromising. I'm rarely fully happy with a decision. I'm rarely fully dissatisfied, either; but being half okay over and over again has begun to wear on me. This time I want it to be about me! Admittedly, I hear the whine factor in these words, but this is a real battle my heart is waging. I get on my kids for wanting their way so often, but the apples truly didn't fall far. I still have areas of selfish stubbornness. Please remind me in a fresh way about the benefits of meeting in the middle, because I'm struggling to appreciate them.

And then . . . I read today's Scripture portion. Verse 2 surprises me as I reread it. Do my efforts to find one mind and purpose with someone else make *you* truly happy? As in *fully satisfied*? Knowing you find pleasure in my desire to live like you is that fresh perspective I need now. Thank you once again for meeting me where I am—and modelling the kind of effort you're looking to see from me.

Make me truly happy by agreeing wholeheartedly with each other, loving one another, and working together with one mind and purpose. Don't be selfish; don't try to impress others. Be humble, thinking of others as better than yourselves.

PHILIPPIANS 2:2-3

DAY 80

☼ A prayer about SALVATION
When I need to be delivered

LORD,

Darkness and despair seem to be the very clothes I wear these days. Often I'm even unsure how to function. In the midst of this trial, I fear I have become a pit dweller. Even though some aspects of this pit can be scary and deep, others feel somewhat comfortable. I cannot see my way forward at this time and am unable to perceive a way of escape.

Even though I feel as though I am drowning in my cares, you are still with me, at the bottom. I need your light, Lord, to shine a pathway so I can find my way out. I need the release of your salvation to deliver me from this hopelessness. Please pull me out of this tiresome pit and plant my feet securely on solid ground. When I rest securely in you, whom can I fear? Lord, you have saved and delivered me. Teach me what glorying in your salvation means and how to share that good news of rescue with others.

The LORD is my light and my salvation—so why should I be afraid? The LORD is my fortress, protecting me from danger, so why should I tremble? PSALM 27:1

☀ **A prayer about JOY**
When I can learn from my child

FATHER,

I will never forget the first time my child laughed. The utter delight on her face brought a new understanding of the word *joy*. She knows she is loved fully and completely, and she delights in the simple things. I want to tap into that joy in my own life and in my relationship with you.

When I stop to count the innumerable blessings you have given me and my family, I am overwhelmed. You have been with me every step of the way, and you continue to shower me with your unfailing love even though I don't deserve it. Thank you for loving me and calling me your child. Help me to learn to trust you the way my child trusts me. Remind me to rejoice in the simple things that you surround me, with like a sunny day or the laughter of a child. Fill my heart with joy and peace today.

You love him even though you have never seen him. Though you do not see him now, you trust him; and you rejoice with a glorious, inexpressible joy. I PETER 1:8

☼ A prayer about PERFECTION
When I can't compete

LORD,

We live in a world of Pinterest, HGTV, and Martha Stewart. At times I feel pressured to live up to some ideal that doesn't come from you. Having an organized house, making baby food from scratch, or giving a homemade themed birthday party are all fine things, but I don't need to do any of these things to be a good mother. I can spend too much time beating myself up for not having the time or energy to do everything everyone else seems to be doing, but you don't want me to compare myself to anyone else.

You have gifted me uniquely and created me just the way I am for a reason. Help me to let go of any preconceived notions of what I think I should be and instead look to you for guidance. Thank you for creating me exactly as I am. Help me to find my worth and self-esteem in you rather than in worldly things.

We are God's masterpiece. He has created us anew in Christ Jesus, so we can do the good things he planned for us long ago.
EPHESIANS 2:10

✺ A prayer about DESTINY
When I think of your sovereign plans

JESUS,

Will you remind me that you have good things in store for me? Sometimes disappointments seem to gang up and wallop me all at once. But no matter what, I can find hope in your promise that you will fulfill your good plans for my life. Thank you for the blessings I trust are coming.

The LORD will work out his plans for my life—for your faithful love, O LORD, endures forever. Don't abandon me, for you made me. PSALM 138:8

DAY 84 *Prayerful Moment*

✺ A prayer about DISAPPOINTMENT
When I need to model healthy ways to handle lost dreams

GOD,

Whether I'm ready or not, my kids will see how I respond to being disappointed. How I handle those times reveals my trust and surrender to your care—or it shows a lack of faith or a spoiled approach to life. Help me to be ready with a gracious, faith-filled response so my children see that I'm resting and rejoicing in you for providing what you know I truly need.

Take delight in the LORD, and he will give you your heart's desires. PSALM 37:4

☼ A prayer about SALVATION
When I feel grateful for life

LORD,

I'm so thankful that you created life! Today I'm going to enjoy reminders of the life you offer. Simply speaking, life lived in you guarantees that you are my Savior, my Redeemer, my hope. You are my joy in the mundane and the tough times, my stability in a mixed-up world. When my strength wears thin, you infuse me with your patient kindness. Your promises carry sweetness beyond this earth. God, you could have abandoned me to a lifetime of despair followed by an eternity separated from you. But you did not. You rescued me through Jesus. I'm going to bask in the comfort that you sent Jesus to save my children as well. I love that you died for me, but I love even more that you died for them.

I praise you for life, for another moment that your Spirit can work in mine, another breath of your refreshing presence so that I may bless my family. Thank you that true life is not limited to how we humans tend to view it. Thank you for salvation, Lord, for defining what life is and for offering it abundantly to us.

The thief's purpose is to steal and kill and destroy. My
purpose is to give them a rich and satisfying life.
JOHN 10:10

※ A prayer about RESPONSIBILITY
When my attitude could use some adjustment

SAVIOR,

My to-do list is a mile long, and I have no idea how everything that I think I need to do today will actually get done. How did all these responsibilities and concerns pile up on top of me? Father, what motivates me to do what I do? Am I striving to live up to standards I have placed upon myself? Or are other people's expectations driving me?

I can tell, Lord, that I have reached the end of myself as I listen to my complaints and desperate cries. I want to quit! To quit trying to do all these duties in my own strength. Lord Jesus, you did only what your Father gave you to do, nothing more and nothing less. You set out to accomplish your Father's will on this earth. So I submit my agendas and task-driven ways to you. Please modify my perspective to pursue what you want to accomplish through me. I want to abandon the desire to work only to please others and have them think well of me. Dear Savior, accomplish your work and will through me for your glory.

Do everything without complaining and arguing.
PHILIPPIANS 2:14

⚙ **A prayer about LOVE**
When I need a model to follow

FATHER,

I am so grateful for the example of love you have given me in the sacrifice of your Son, Jesus. You loved me so much that you sent him to this earth so that I would have forgiveness and a close, personal relationship with you. I want to teach my children how to love as you have loved me.

Help me exhibit your love to my children by giving me your patience and kindness. Help me show them who you are through my words and actions today. Thank you for giving me a glimpse of what your love for me looks like in the way I feel toward my children.

Love is patient and kind. Love is not jealous or boastful or proud or rude. It does not demand its own way. It is not irritable, and it keeps no record of being wronged. It does not rejoice about injustice but rejoices whenever the truth wins out. Love never gives up, never loses faith, is always hopeful, and endures through every circumstance.

I CORINTHIANS 13:4-7

☼ A prayer about ABSENCE
When I feel myself withdraw

LORD,

At times I'm not truly present with my children, even though I'm with them. Sometimes I must seem unreachable when my thoughts are distant from them. While it's true that they can "Mother, Mother, MOTHER!" me to near insanity, sometimes I'm just somewhere else despite being in the same room. I guess it is possible to be an absentee mother even when I'm home.

If my heart feels anxious or my schedule is packed, I feel my mind going on a hiatus to escape from the demands for a while. I want to be reliable and present for them; they need to know that Mother will be Mother today and tomorrow, and they won't have to shout on a regular basis to get my attention. Father, strengthen me to be truly with them as much as they need me, and awaken them to respect my personhood as well. Help me to balance my interests that need attention too. Will you grow understanding and healthy independence in my kids so they respect my need for space to regroup now and then? And please keep me from retreating into absentee-mother mode.

No, I will not abandon you as orphans—I will come to you.
JOHN 14:18

☀ A prayer about TENDERNESS
When I need a fresh outpouring of grace

HOLY SPIRIT,

My walk with you has been stale. My soul is left parched from incessant activity. My relational well has run dry, and I feel as though I have nothing to offer loved ones, friends, and neighbors. I need a fresh outpouring of you in my life. Give me moments to drink in your grace. I need your refreshing presence from early in the morning to late at night. Your tender nourishment is essential to my growth in Christlikeness. After years of pointless effort, I know I cannot give to others what I have not first received from you.

Keep me saturated in gospel truth so that I will not return to this aimless pursuit. Holy Spirit, please fill me with your fruits of joy, peace, patience, love, and self-control. As these virtues soak into my life, may they overflow into my relationships. Convict me of areas that have been hardened by sin. Remove attitudes that quench your work in my life. Refresh me with your tender compassion today that I might be a spring of life to those I love.

Let my teaching fall on you like rain; let my speech settle like dew. Let my words fall like rain on tender grass, like gentle showers on young plants. DEUTERONOMY 32:2

☼ **A prayer about HURTS**
  When I can't fix them

HEAVENLY FATHER,

Today my child is hurting. The world can be cruel, and I want to take away his pain and make it better. But not every hurt is something I can fix with a hug or a cookie. Please be with my child in the midst of the pain, and work even this bad thing together with your plan for good in his life.

We know that God causes everything to work together for the good of those who love God and are called according to his purpose for them. ROMANS 8:28

DAY 91 *Prayerful Moment*

☼ **A prayer about PRIORITIES**
  When I pursue the many things over the one thing

LORD,

As I consider all the tasks before me today, my heart is restless, and I struggle to know how to be still before you. Lord, give me grace to sit close and listen to your Word. Forgive me for the many times I tie my worth in your eyes to productivity rather than to devotion to you.

There is only one thing worth being concerned about. Mary has discovered it, and it will not be taken away from her. LUKE 10:42

☼ A prayer about INFLUENCES
When I want to protect my child

LORD JESUS,

Bad influences can creep into my child's life in so many ways. The proliferation of technology and the easy availability of the Internet have made it very difficult for me to keep him sheltered from the ugliness of the world. I want to guard my child from seeing and hearing things that he is too young to understand, knowing that once something is seen, it can't be unseen. I could spend all of my time worrying and trying to block every possible negative force from his life, but I don't think that is what you desire for me or for him.

Help me to know how to teach my child to be a light in this dark world without withdrawing from it or being afraid of it. Show me how to appropriately guard his heart while still allowing him to grow up and experience the world. May he learn to make wise decisions about what he allows to enter his mind. Thank you for being an example of how to live in a sinful world.

Don't copy the behavior and customs of this world, but let God transform you into a new person by changing the way you think. Then you will learn to know God's will for you, which is good and pleasing and perfect. ROMANS 12:2

☼ A prayer about CONTENTMENT
When I feel restless in my circumstances

FATHER,

I struggle to model contentment consistently to my kids. I tell them to choose to be happy, not to compare themselves to others, to be grateful for what they have . . . and then I catch my thoughts and eyes wandering to ways my life feels lacking. Minor happenings can chip away at my contentment. A visit with a friend may start me wishing for her nicer home or for hair like hers. Those thoughts can set me to wondering how I could improve my figure or find more career success or encourage my husband to help around the house.

It's exhausting, Lord, which surely is why you warn us against falling into discontent. But Lord, it can be difficult to remain logical about real troubles and not let my emotions take over. How do I admit true feelings but not let them get me down? I don't want the cancer of jealousy to rot my spirit. Please flood me with yourself and help me to remember that, as your daughter, I have all the riches of your wealth and all the love of your heart.

A peaceful heart leads to a healthy body; jealousy is like cancer in the bones. PROVERBS 14:30

✿ **A prayer about BUSYNESS**
When I forget to slow down

JESUS,

Why do I get so consumed with the day-to-day tasks of motherhood that I forget you are quietly walking with me? The demands that immediately fill my mind each morning tend to drown out your gentle voice. You are longing for me to turn to you and talk to you. You patiently wait for me to remember that you are always there. You are never too busy for me. Why do I always seem to be too busy for you?

Today help me remember how important it is that you are with me—all day, every day. You are always available to listen, to advise . . . even to share lighthearted moments with. I don't need to rush through life jumping from one task to another. Remind me that you will bring rest to my soul and renew my energy if I let you. Thank you, Jesus, for doing life with me and for being with me every day.

O people, the LORD has told you what is good, and this is what he requires of you: to do what is right, to love mercy, and to walk humbly with your God. MICAH 6:8

☀ **A prayer about COURAGE**
When I need to remember it isn't all up to me

ALMIGHTY GOD,

Thank you for possessing every ounce of courage I need. Thank you also for promising to make up for everything I don't have in order to accomplish your goals. Relying on you will be one of the ongoing lessons of my life. Why does it take such gutsiness for me to stop spinning my wheels, cease scrambling to come up with my own solutions, and simply let go and rest in your unwavering courage? You never doubt your ability to be enough for me. Please help me grow my courage in you more than trying to fabricate it in myself.

Impress on me each day that my forced efforts are in vain. You hold the power; you hold the bravery; and you ensure the victory when I make room in my spirit for yours to move in and fill me. Father, my kids need to see what relying on you looks like, so please help me to grow and show—to grow in my own reliance on you and to show them what a life empowered by you looks like. *By your Spirit.* May that be my life's message.

It is not by force nor by strength, but by my Spirit, says the LORD of Heaven's Armies. ZECHARIAH 4:6

☀ **A prayer about DEPRESSION**
When I have trouble admitting I need help

FATHER,

I may be the last to see it, but I'm finally here to admit I can't fix this. I want to be strong. I want to shed this shroud of depression on my own. I should be able to do that, right? But then I read a psalm like the one today, and I don't feel so inadequate. Or at least I don't feel so alone in it. Those psalmists held nothing back from you. They admitted when life was too much.

I know in my head that depression is not about weak or strong. It actually takes a great deal of strength to carry that weight every moment, every day. But my heart still fights to hold my own. Maybe I've needed to learn to let the pieces fall so you can show me how you put them back together even better. I need you to fill me and point me to people and resources that can help me. Lord, please address my feelings of shame about this battle. Right now, I choose to rest in you and let you open the path of healing. I'm yours.

Come quickly, LORD, and answer me, for my depression deepens. . . . Let me hear of your unfailing love each morning, for I am trusting you. Show me where to walk, for I give myself to you. PSALM 143:7-8

☀ **A prayer about STRESS**
When I need deliverance from anxieties

LORD,

Everywhere I turn I feel squeezed and crushed by the weight of my concerns. Anxieties about the uncertainties of life crowd my every thought. I need rescue from above. Please deliver me, Lord, from my troubled perspective. Guide me into days that are filled with joy and contentment. I surrender to your plan, which is far better than I could ever hope or imagine.

Do not snatch your word of truth from me, for your regulations are my only hope. PSALM 119:43

DAY 98 *Prayerful Moment*

☀ **A prayer about NEEDS**
When I need to be thankful

LORD,

You have promised to provide for all of my needs, yet I spend so much time worrying. Help me learn to trust you fully with my life and be grateful for what I have rather than complain about what I don't have.

Don't worry about these things, saying, "What will we eat? What will we drink? What will we wear?" These things dominate the thoughts of unbelievers, but your heavenly Father already knows all your needs. MATTHEW 6:31-32

☀ A prayer about MARRIAGE
When I want the best home life for my child

GOD,

I am sad when I look around at the world today and see what has become of your design for marriage. You have created us to be in community with each other. You've designed marriage to be an intimate connection. But sin has come in and messed up what you so lovingly created. The world is full of destroyed relationships, casual sex, and lack of commitment. I don't want this and the heartbreak it could mean for my children. I want them to experience the full joy of marriage the way you designed it to be.

Help me teach my children the values of honesty, commitment, and intimacy that are the foundations of a healthy marriage. Guide them in making wise choices as they grow and begin to look for a mate. Provide them with healthy examples of godly marriages.

The LORD God made a woman from the rib, and he brought her to the man. "At last!" the man exclaimed. "This one is bone from my bone, and flesh from my flesh! She will be called 'woman,' because she was taken from 'man.'" This explains why a man leaves his father and mother and is joined to his wife, and the two are united into one.
GENESIS 2:22-24

☀ A prayer about COMMITMENT
When I want to encourage perseverance

LORD,

Music lessons, homework assignments, household chores, sports practice . . . what do these have in common? All require commitment and discipline, and all are things my kids could be tempted to bail on. I get that they're kids. Their maturity isn't adult-sized yet, so their struggle to finish challenging tasks is understandable. But how do I know when and how to push—or rather, to *encourage* them to keep on keeping on? I don't want them to adopt the common lifestyle of taking the easy way out. They need to see themselves press through to reach a goal—even if the reward is the simple satisfaction of doing their best or experiencing character growth.

Please help my children learn the value of commitment on their level. We may be talking about skimping on piano practice now, but failing to grow in commitment could translate into skipping out on a difficult marriage or a healthy lifestyle later on. They need to benefit from the discipline of seeing themselves work through hard things when they're young. Thanks, Father, for your commitment to help us learn together.

I have fought the good fight, I have finished the race, and I have remained faithful. 2 TIMOTHY 4:7

DAY 101

☀ A prayer about OBSTACLES
When I can't find my way

LORD,

Just when I think I have discerned your will and where I need to go, I find myself facing roadblocks and closed doors. I should not be surprised by this, as I know the enemy wants to discourage me from following you. Help me knock down the walls that are surrounding me and persevere to find a way around the barriers. Remind me that you have a plan for me and promise to walk with me through the dark valleys. I am not alone on this journey, and I need only to call out to you for help when I feel discouraged or alone.

Thank you for standing with me and being my refuge when I feel like I am being attacked and thwarted from following the path you have for me. Give me the strength to continue to push forward when it feels too difficult. Guide my feet and clear the way for me to take the next step.

Joyful are people of integrity, who follow the instructions of the LORD. Joyful are those who obey his laws and search for him with all their hearts. They do not compromise with evil, and they walk only in his paths. You have charged us to keep your commandments carefully. Oh, that my actions would consistently reflect your decrees! PSALM 119:1-5

☼ A prayer about WITNESSING
When I long to see the light of the gospel spread

ALMIGHTY GOD,

I feel as though you have called us to live in this community. I have thoroughly enjoyed getting to know our neighbors and having them over. I so desperately want them all to know of your saving love. May your grace shine so brightly in our home that others will realize that your presence makes all the difference. Then, as you give us opportunities to love and serve our neighbors, may they see how our faith motivates us and impacts our choices. May our home shine as a lamp not only to our neighbors but also into our surrounding community.

Please help me link arms with brothers and sisters in Christ and remember to pray consistently for my town and nation to know you. Remind me when my world gets too small that you are the King over all the nations. I want to pray, give, and go so that your gospel may extend to the ends of the earth.

You will receive power when the Holy Spirit comes upon you. And you will be my witnesses, telling people about me everywhere—in Jerusalem, throughout Judea, in Samaria, and to the ends of the earth. ACTS 1:8

☀ **A prayer about the HOLY SPIRIT**
When I am lonely

HOLY SPIRIT,

Being a mother can sometimes feel so isolating. I love being with my child, but I can feel very alone. When I need to be rejuvenated, I am so grateful for your presence. You never leave me and are waiting to fill me up with your strength and power—I need only to ask.

Thank you for your presence in my life, even when I forget and try to do things in my own power. Thank you for knowing what I need, even when I do not. Thank you for refreshing me, sometimes in unexpected ways. Thank you for never leaving me to deal with life alone.

I will ask the Father, and he will give you another Advocate, who will never leave you. He is the Holy Spirit, who leads into all truth. The world cannot receive him, because it isn't looking for him and doesn't recognize him. But you know him, because he lives with you now and later will be in you.
JOHN 14:16-17

☼ **A prayer about REWARD**
When I am impatient for results

FATHER,

I gave that project my best shot, and now I am just waiting to see the results. Like a farmer watching for the first sprouts to appear, I must wait for the outcome. Help me to wait well, Lord, knowing that I am modeling the virtues of patience and delayed gratification to my children. During this time, help both my kids and me to better understand the benefits of persevering and waiting on you.

Wise words bring many benefits, and hard work brings rewards. PROVERBS 12:14

DAY 105 *Prayerful Moment*

☼ **A prayer about GRIEF**
When I have experienced loss

LORD,

You have promised me that you will always be with me. As waves of sorrow wash over me, I need you now more than ever before. Hold me in your arms and comfort me. Remind me that you are my ever-present help in trouble. Thank you for never leaving me.

The LORD is close to the brokenhearted; he rescues those whose spirits are crushed. PSALM 34:18

☼ **A prayer about MERCY**
When I appreciate your grace

HEAVENLY FATHER,

There is something amazing about watching my little girl learn to interact with and care about the people around her. She has gone from being unaware of others' needs to being concerned about their feelings and noticing when someone feels left out.

I realize that I still have so much to learn about your heart and how you see the world, but I am so grateful for how you are showing me new ways to experience compassion and mercy through my child's eyes. Help me to catch her being kind so that I can affirm the compassion I see in her. And may she learn to look to you for grace and compassion whenever she stumbles or loses her way.

With all my heart I will praise you, O Lord my God. I will give glory to your name forever, for your love for me is very great. . . . You, O Lord, are a God of compassion and mercy, slow to get angry and filled with unfailing love and faithfulness. PSALM 86:12-13, 15

☼ A prayer about EMOTIONS
When mine demand too much of me

LORD,

These emotions are too much for me. They're climbing all over my insides, clamoring like big apes for more, more, more attention. They're wearing me out and leaving me reactive instead of stable and responsive. It's hard to do the daily tasks of life well when my emotions lead the way and run ragged over everyone in my life. Is there any respite from their intensity? I fear that I'm showing my children how to live according to emotions, a recipe for disaster. Feelings are important and necessary, and I'd be wrong to ignore them. But they cannot have free rein if I'm to set a consistent, well-adjusted example as a mother.

Lord, you have revealed yourself as Healer and Savior and Emmanuel, God with us. I need you to be my Balancer as well. Heal me of ravenous emotions. Be bigger than they are, Jesus, when they threaten to swallow me. Steady me with your own balanced Spirit, and help me to set the example of putting feelings in their place of helpfulness instead of allowing them to hinder me and the well-being of my family.

You are controlled by the Spirit if you have the Spirit of God living in you. ROMANS 8:9

DAY 108

☀ A prayer about SACRIFICE
When I need pure motivations

FATHER,

Today I am feeling the cost of motherhood. Every moment seems to bring a new occasion to give of my time, energy, and resources. Many days seem to have unlimited requests. I know that I do not possess limitless resources to give to others. And I confess that I often feel depleted and empty. Sometimes I resent the demands on my life. Other times I pride myself in how self-sacrificially I give myself to others. I know, Lord, that all these sacrifices mean nothing if I do not first sacrifice my heart to you.

So I repent of thinking that my efforts to work harder for others are what truly please you. I know your love for me does not depend on how much I work and sacrifice. Father, what you desire from me is a broken and contrite heart. Please help me see the demands of the day as opportunities to present to you a woman who is devoted to becoming more conformed to your likeness.

Purify me from my sins, and I will be clean; wash me, and I will be whiter than snow. PSALM 51:7

☼ A prayer about VALUES
When I place worth on outward behavior

GOD,

Today my son began talking about the core values he is learning at school. Hearing him talk about integrity, honesty, and character has been fascinating. Society highly prizes these values and considers them important to be taught. We usually forget, however, that all of these virtues are deeply rooted in your character and cannot be fully understood apart from knowing you. I want my children to display these values, but I confess I am rarely willing to do the hard work of discipleship with them.

The real issue is not how we behave on the outside but rather what motivates and compels us from the inside. What do we value most as a family? I seem to find my worth in so many things, so am I really willing to say that nothing is more valuable than knowing you? Help me use these conversations as a corrective for our family to give you first place in everything.

Everything else is worthless when compared with the infinite value of knowing Christ Jesus my Lord. For his sake I have discarded everything else, counting it all as garbage, so that I could gain Christ. PHILIPPIANS 3:8

⚘ **A prayer about ROLE MODELS**
When I need someone to follow

GOD,

I so desire for my children to have excellent role models. I want them to have men and women in their lives who follow hard after you. I pray that you would divinely ordain interesting interactions and challenging conversations throughout their week. Thank you for the time and talents that these mentors graciously give to others.

May you give my children eyes to see how these individuals' faith impacts every area of their lives. May you give them ears to listen to the words of wisdom from those who are further along the way in their spiritual walks. May you give them hands to serve alongside these people, discovering what their God-given gifts and abilities really are. May you give them feet to apply these truths and walk them out by faith. Thank you, Lord, for the body of Christ and their godly examples in my children's lives.

Live a life filled with love, following the example of Christ. He loved us and offered himself as a sacrifice for us, a pleasing aroma to God. EPHESIANS 5:2

⚜ **A prayer about APPROVAL**
   When my child needs to thrive in your acceptance

LORD,

It hurts to see my child work so hard for approval from others. Like most of us, she obviously feels validated when others notice her, but what a trap that can become! Please fill her with the secure confidence that comes from knowing that she is your unique creation. Remind her that she doesn't need to strive to make someone's "approved" list. Help her find her value in you.

Thank you for making me so wonderfully complex! Your workmanship is marvelous—how well I know it.
PSALM 139:14

⚜ **A prayer about HOME**
   When I am grateful

LORD JESUS,

Your Word reminds me that you had no earthly home of your own. I know that even now many of your followers around the globe struggle to find adequate shelter. I am so blessed that you have provided a safe haven for our family. Forgive us for those times when we take it for granted or even envy those with bigger homes or "better" possessions.

They were looking for a better place, a heavenly homeland. That is why God is not ashamed to be called their God, for he has prepared a city for them. HEBREWS 11:16

DAY 113

☼ A prayer about ACCOMPLISHMENTS
When I feel unproductive

LORD,

I didn't get very far this morning before I started feeling insecure about what I get done each day—or rather, what I *don't* get done. Every morning I wake up wanting to accomplish this and that, but most every evening I go to bed feeling weighed down by all I couldn't cross off my list. Oh, to finish my to-dos, even once or twice a week!

I look around at other women who seem to do so much—manage a career, run a household, help with homework, volunteer at school, show up at the kids' activities—and on time, too! I value so much about this season of life, Father, and I know my desire to love my family the best I can is honorable. But sometimes I'd like to see tangible results—and yes, even receive a little thanks—for all I do. Please help me shed my layers of doubt and shine your truth into my heart. I need your help to remember that in your book my highest accomplishment is living as an example of your love, truth, and grace each day.

Be an example . . . in what you say, in the way you live, in your love, your faith, and your purity. 1 TIMOTHY 4:12

☼ A prayer about CONFLICT
When forgiveness comes hard

GOD,

My kids see this conflict I'm in. They know I've been hurt, and that bothers them. And whether they're conscious of it or not, they will see me model one of two things: hanging on to a grudge or forgiving when it's hard. Father, I know I've got to forgive so my heart is right, but also so the lesson is not lost on my children. I want to inspire them, to be able to speak Philippians 4:9 without shame or hesitation, knowing you're pleased with how I'm managing this issue.

Are my children witnessing my forgiving heart in action? Am I taking the lead with a pure heart even if the other person doesn't respect me or share my desire to honor you? These are weighty burdens, God. But I will have no peace unless I give them to you and move forward in the direction of forgiveness. When I obey your ways, I will experience your peace despite this conflict, and I will also enjoy your peace that comes from knowing I've done well for my kids' growth. Please help me, because I'll fail on my own. Thank you, Lord.

Keep putting into practice all you learned and received from me—everything you heard from me and saw me doing. Then the God of peace will be with you. PHILIPPIANS 4:9

☀ A prayer about MEANING
When I need to feel significant

LORD,

So many times I find myself feeling as though I have no worth. I go about my day and check tasks off my list—doing dishes, running errands, folding clothes—only to go to bed and wake up and do it all over again. It is so easy to feel that what I do doesn't matter and then spiral into depression.

But you see all that I do every day, and not only do you recognize it as worthy, you see how it fits into the bigger picture. You have given me gifts and talents that fit into your grand design. You take all that I do, even the little things, and work them together to help accomplish your plan. Remind me that I am building into the lives of my children. Thank you for seeing all that I do and for giving me the energy to keep going each day.

What is the price of two sparrows—one copper coin? But not a single sparrow can fall to the ground without your Father knowing it. And the very hairs on your head are all numbered. So don't be afraid; you are more valuable to God than a whole flock of sparrows. MATTHEW 10:29-31

☼ A prayer about the BIBLE
When I need the changing power of your Word

LORD,

I'm counting on you to move in me through your Word. Right now I'm pressed to meet many demands, and the stress is taking a toll on my sense of calm. You've let me know in the past that my greatest strength often results from taking a couple of minutes to soak up your energy in your Word, no matter what else is going on—*especially* when there's so much going on. More of you means less chaos inside me.

Please bless this expenditure of time reading your Word as I count on your messages to sink into my spirit. Expand my heart, tame the circumstances, and smooth the rough spots within and without that push me to panic. Reveal strains of selfishness and impatience in me, and equip me to handle life with more Christlikeness. Your Word is mighty, like you are, Lord. Thank you for offering all your power to me. May your Word produce your fruit in me and through me.

All Scripture is inspired by God and is useful to teach us what is true and to make us realize what is wrong in our lives. It corrects us when we are wrong and teaches us to do what is right. God uses it to prepare and equip his people to do every good work. 2 TIMOTHY 3:16-17

☀ A prayer about AVAILABILITY
When I see so many needs around me

GOD,

Opening the mail this week reminded me of so many needs. Globally, nationally, locally, even right in my neighborhood and family, hearts are hurting. I wish I had the power and availability to fix them all. But that's not what you ask of me. You don't ask me to singlehandedly save your world—not in my lifetime, not this year, and certainly not by noon.

Sometimes I overlook the daily gifts of grace and availability that I can offer. When I forget to act as your hands and feet in everyday moments, remind me that you ask me to do what is right and to love mercy. Align my focus on those goals so I will continually notice opportunities to extend hope and healing. Keep my heart available for someone who needs even just a warm smile or an affirming word. Maybe I don't trust enough that where you place me each day is exactly where I'll find the needs you want me to meet. Please help me to live mercifully and fully for you right now. And the next right now and the next one and the next . . .

The LORD has told you what is good, and this is what he requires of you: to do what is right, to love mercy, and to walk humbly with your God. MICAH 6:8

❄ **A prayer about SAFETY**
When I need a way of escape

HEAVENLY FATHER,

Thank you that even as I reread a favorite Bible story with my child, I can be reminded of your watchful care. Just as you closed Noah and his family safely in the ark, you surround my family with your faithfulness. Help me rejoice that we, too, will be guided safely to places of new beginnings.

A male and female of each kind entered, just as God had commanded Noah. Then the LORD closed the door behind them. GENESIS 7:16

DAY 119 *Prayerful Moment*

❄ **A prayer about SELF-ESTEEM**
When I want to build up my children

JESUS,

Forgive me for my quick and angry words today. Next time, help me to pause and pray before I open my mouth. I want to build up my children, not tear them down. I know words have the power to bring life or death to them. Give me your words to both shape and support them to believe the truest things that can be said of them as found in your Word.

Encourage each other and build each other up, just as you are already doing. 1 THESSALONIANS 5:11

☼ A prayer about DISCIPLINE
When I need to remember loving correction

FATHER GOD,

I'm so grateful that you don't clobber me over the head or shame me when I make a mess of things. Those responses would tear me up because most times I want to do right despite the problem of my humanness.

My humanness comes through in my mistakes as a parent, too. Lord, I need frequent reminders to follow your positive, encouraging method of discipline with my own children. They're great kids, but their behavior can be maddening at times, and I struggle to hold back negative reactions. Yet I'm pretty sure there's got to be a more inspiring way to grow them up than by spewing my anger and frustration in their direction.

When I must admonish my children, help me to do so with a calm mind and a loving heart. Your Word tells me that when I discipline them appropriately, I will gain peace of mind and gladness. I can't help wondering whether that has a boomerang effect: maybe when I correct their behavior while affirming their worth and my heartfelt delight in them as people, they, too, will enjoy peace of mind and joyful hearts.

Please help me handle their hearts with sensitivity, wisdom, and grace today.

Discipline your children, and they will give you peace of mind and will make your heart glad. PROVERBS 29:17

⚙ **A prayer about HOME**
When I need perspective

LORD,

I want my home to be a sanctuary for my family. Having a perfectly decorated or spotless house is not the goal, although I can be easily distracted by the need to show off. I want to create a place where my family feels safe and secure. A place where they can be themselves without fear of judgment. A place where they can rejuvenate their bodies and souls. I want it to be obvious to everyone who comes in that you dwell here with us.

You are the heartbeat of our home. I want your love and grace to permeate this house each day and spill out to bless all those we come in contact with. Help me to create this kind of home for my family—one that reflects your Spirit.

Jesus replied, "All who love me will do what I say. My Father will love them, and we will come and make our home with each of them." JOHN 14:23

☼ A prayer about PERSPECTIVE
When I need to remember what is truly important

HEAVENLY FATHER,

Being a mother can be overwhelming and exhausting. On days like that I can begin to feel sorry for myself. Then a news story or a prayer request reminds me that so many mothers around the world are dealing with circumstances that I can't even begin to understand: mothers who can't afford to feed, clothe, or house their children, even mothers who are not sure if their child will live through the day. Famine, disease, heartache, and pain are a part of this fallen world.

But you, Father, have come to bring hope and healing to all who struggle in this life. You have given me more blessings each day than I can count. Thank you for loving me and providing for me today. Help me to remember that you are my hope and healer.

Love never gives up, never loses faith, is always hopeful, and endures through every circumstance.

I CORINTHIANS 13:7

☼ A prayer about WORK
When I must juggle home and work responsibilities

LORD,

These days I feel as if I need to make every second count.
Getting my family out the door every morning feels like a
race against the clock. Can I serve breakfast, make lunches,
and sign that stray school permission slip before the bus
comes? Then will I be able to meet my boss's expectations
on the job and still pick up my kids from after-school practice on time? At home, my mind often wanders to the
growing pile in my in-box; at work, I often wish *I* could
be the one reading to my preschooler and then settling her
down for her nap.

Lord, help me to keep focused on wherever I happen to
be at every moment, trusting you to supply my kids' needs
and to give me the creativity and stamina I need each day
at work. Help me resist the temptation to try to be super-
mother or superwoman. May I, instead, find true joy and
contentment in using my gifts—however imperfectly—to
serve other people and point them to you.

*Pay careful attention to your own work, for then you will
get the satisfaction of a job well done, and you won't need to
compare yourself to anyone else.* GALATIANS 6:4

☼ A prayer about CHARACTER
When I need to teach that integrity begins on the inside

LORD,

It all begins in the mind, doesn't it? Every choice a person makes, for good or bad, begins with one thought. As I watch my children conduct themselves—and even when I am not with them to provide accountability—please help me to show them that character begins on the inside. Character goes deeper than behavior. Anyone can play a role for a while, but eventually the true person comes out.

Please sensitize their hearts to desire solid character that comes from following you. I pray their integrity will shine and they will have the boldness to do what is right even when their peers are going in another direction. Grow them as faithful followers of you and compassionate leaders of people. And Father, please help my character to impact my parenting so that they are drawn to you instead of feeling suffocated by lots of dos and don'ts. Character needs to be a heart thing, or it really is nothing.

Fix your thoughts on what is true, and honorable, and right, and pure, and lovely, and admirable. Think about things that are excellent and worthy of praise. PHILIPPIANS 4:8

✿ A prayer about BELONGING
When my children try too hard to fit in

FATHER,

I cringe when I see my kids try so hard to be accepted by their peers. I understand their emotions because even I still experience fear of rejection at times. Please show my children that their worth and their purpose are solidified by belonging to you. Guard their hearts and minds when other pressures tempt them to waste their emotions and integrity trying to please other people more than you. And please will you help them learn this lesson while they're young?

They loved human praise more than the praise of God.
JOHN 12:43

DAY 126 *Prayerful Moment*

✿ A prayer about INFERTILITY
When words are not enough

LORD,

My friend came to me in tears today. Month after month, she's been disappointed. My heart breaks for her and for all those who mourn the loss of their unborn children or their barren wombs. Bring comfort to my friend and to others facing infertility today. Hear their cry and be their strength.

He has not ignored or belittled the suffering of the needy. He has not turned his back on them, but has listened to their cries for help. PSALM 22:24

☼ A prayer about SPIRITUAL GROWTH
When I need to flourish and mature

GOD,

Thank you for the opportunity to work in the garden. I love to be close to your creation and reminded of how you sustain life. I wrestled with one too many weeds today, and my back will not let me forget it. It is amazing to see how entangled and deep their roots go. The very presence of weeds impacts the well-being of all my other plants.

Please cause me, Lord, to be deeply rooted in you, building my life upon the truths found in the pages of your Word. May your ongoing sanctifying work in me cause my faith to develop and grow. Saturate my mind and heart with your truth. God, I want my life to be not only healthy but also fruitful. May the strength of my spiritual walk impact my children and their friends. Uproot my sinful behaviors and attitudes. My goal, Lord, is to seek to grow with an eye toward maturity.

Let your roots grow down into him, and let your lives be built on him. Then your faith will grow strong in the truth you were taught, and you will overflow with thankfulness.
COLOSSIANS 2:7

❁ A prayer about WITNESSING
When I try to draw others out in faith conversations

LORD,

I find the conversations that circulate around the lunch table at work very interesting. People continually reveal the conditions of their hearts by their words. I know you have divinely placed me in this company to be a witness for the gospel.

Please use the words of my mouth to cause others to crave a relationship with you. Make me a *salty* woman who helps others thirst for truth. Give me wisdom and discernment as I consider how to draw out people in conversations. Sprinkle my words with grace and love that I might win my brothers and sisters. Help me to prioritize time in your Word in order to saturate my mind with your truth. Prepare my heart so that I might always be ready to give an answer for the hope that lies within me.

You are the salt of the earth. But what good is salt if it has lost its flavor? Can you make it salty again? It will be thrown out and trampled underfoot as worthless.

MATTHEW 5:13

⚜ **A prayer about PURPOSE**
  When I am lost in transition

FATHER,

I feel lost today in the midst of many transitions. In this new season of life, I have so many possibilities to choose from. The real question before me is, whose direction will I follow? Help me to seek you first. Forgive me when people, possessions, and other priorities compete for first place in my affections. Show me what being zealous and intentional means, as I desire to do your will.

Father, would you rule and reign in my heart in such a way that I would never again be tempted to try to dethrone you? I want to live a life that is pleasing to you. I thank you for your promise that as I endeavor to seek you above all else, you will give me everything I need. Help me forsake my cravings for self-indulgence. Lord, I know as I get this established in my heart, you will show me what your best purposes are for me in this new stage of life.

Seek the Kingdom of God above all else, and live righteously, and he will give you everything you need.
MATTHEW 6:33

☼ A prayer about NEEDS
When I feel overwhelmed

HEAVENLY FATHER,

I need only look at the latest news report or parenting magazine to feel as if I can mess up as a mother in so many ways. But then I can become paralyzed with the fear of doing or saying the wrong thing. I know that you don't want me to live in fear of mistakes I might make. You want me to live in constant surrender to your will and to trust that you will help me raise my child in a loving home. The fact is, I will make mistakes. But you can work all things together for good. You love my child and have a good plan for his life.

Thank you for giving me this little life to raise together with you. Help me to look to you for guidance every day as I navigate motherhood. Thank you for walking this journey with me and entrusting this precious life to me.

Don't be afraid, for I am with you. Don't be discouraged, for I am your God. I will strengthen you and help you. I will hold you up with my victorious right hand.
ISAIAH 41:10

☼ **A prayer about PEACE**
When I need a tranquil moment

O LORD,

In the middle of the night, the house is quiet. I love to peek in on my sleeping children and see the peaceful innocence on their faces. My heart bursts with love for them, and the worries of the day fade away. If only I could bottle this serenity and pull it out during the daylight hours, when I feel harried and frazzled and at the end of my rope.

You, Lord, have promised to bring me rest and peace. You have promised to shoulder my burdens and lighten my load. Help me to let you bring me to restful green pastures. Restore my soul, as you have promised you will. Remind me in the middle of my frantic busyness that you are my shepherd and all I need to do is follow you.

The LORD is my shepherd; I have all that I need. He lets me rest in green meadows; he leads me beside peaceful streams. He renews my strength. He guides me along right paths, bringing honor to his name. PSALM 23:1-3

DAY 132 *Prayerful Moment*

☀ **A prayer about WEARINESS**
When I am prompted to surrender to your power

JESUS,

Our daughter is in trouble again. Our hearts are sick and weary. We are done trying to fix the situation—we surrender to your will. Only you can rescue and restore her faith. She has always belonged to you. You love and know her far better than we do. We come to you with our tears and prayers, asking you to draw her close. Give us just the right words and wisdom when we speak with her next.

You guide me with your counsel, leading me to a glorious destiny. PSALM 73:24

DAY 133 *Prayerful Moment*

☀ **A prayer about NEIGHBORS**
When I need to reach out

LORD,

You have placed me in this community for a reason. You know each and every one of my neighbors by name. You have a plan for them. Help me to see them through your eyes, and show me how you want to use me in their lives today. For those who are lonely, may I reflect your love. For those who are burdened, may I mirror your grace.

I was hungry, and you fed me. I was thirsty, and you gave me a drink. I was a stranger, and you invited me into your home. MATTHEW 25:35

☀ A prayer about CONFLICT
When I'm tempted to shrink back from tension

LORD,

How I love peace! Tension is not my cup of tea, so I avoid conflict. Lord, you value peace too because you talk so much about it in your Word. It seems to me that a healthier view of living in peace can provide the gumption I need to stand strong and gracious in the midst of conflict.

Jesus, you set the example of working for peace. Peace does not mean giving in to a bully or a mistruth to avoid an argument. Peacekeeping oftentimes requires peacemaking. Being peaceful means struggling through something difficult or threatening for the benefit of something greater. I love your promise to bless those who work for peace. You give me permission to stand strong. You even help me to live in your power as your child when I do the hard work required to stand up for your ways. Thank you that I don't need to give in to fear. You desire much more for me. By your grace and power I will work for peace even when it means the tension is heightened for a while.

God blesses those who work for peace, for they will be called the children of God. MATTHEW 5:9

☼ A prayer about RISK
When I fear the unknown

GOD,

I confess that I am risk averse. The uncertainty of the unknown often paralyzes me. I am fearful of trying new things and entering into new relationships. I see too much potential for disappointment and failure. What if things don't work out? What if the people involved don't like me? Lord, I fear I have missed out on blessings that could have been mine had I only trusted that you would be there as I stepped into the unknown. Please show me the hidden recesses of my heart where fear needs to be replaced with faith. Help me to walk by faith and not by sight.

You have prepared a path for my life, and now you are calling me to move forward, confident in your best for me. Show me opportunities to trust you in the events that lie before me. Give me direction and guidance to navigate the strange and unfamiliar roads before me. Challenge me to believe that as I step out, you will always be there to go before me and behind me, hemming me in with your love.

We live by believing and not by seeing.
2 CORINTHIANS 5:7

☀ A prayer about OPPORTUNITIES
When I need to be bold

LORD,

I am burdened for my family members who do not yet know the freedom that comes from following you. I want each of them to know what it's like to walk with you and trust you with their lives. I know that you desire each person to turn to you, and I know that I have a part to play in fulfilling that goal.

Sometimes I am too timid to talk about you with my unsaved family because I am afraid of pushing them away or worry what they might think of me. Help me to put my fears aside and share my faith with the confidence that can only come from you. Help me to make the most of every opportunity you present to me and not walk away with regrets about what I could have said. Remind me to continually lift up my unsaved family in prayer, knowing that you will hear and answer me. Help me to be patient with the process and not get discouraged if I don't see immediate results. Thank you for saving me and for desiring a close relationship with every person you've created.

The Lord isn't really being slow about his promise, as some people think. No, he is being patient for your sake. He does not want anyone to be destroyed, but wants everyone to repent. 2 PETER 3:9

☼ **A prayer about FATIGUE**
When your strength is revealed in my weakness

LORD,

How I'd love to cast off fatigue like worn-out clothing. Imagine that freedom. Imagine that strength now, when I feel so depleted. Lord, I love how you flip reality on its head with your better way. You take weary, overdone human beings and show that you want to be strong for us. Please do that wonder in me today, Lord. I'm ready. I'm willing. And I'm tired of being tired. I want to be able to speak today's verse from personal experience, so help me focus on your enabling power. Quiet the noise in my spirit with your holy hush.

What would it feel like to thrive victoriously when I feel at my lowest? Please glorify your great name by doing something new in and through me. I'm yours now, all my best and all my worst. Make yourself known in this story you're giving me to live. Thank you, Lord, for what you're doing and what you're going to do to prove that you're the God of the new. The Lord of the weary. The rebuilder of the broken. Please, let's be victorious together today.

I will strengthen you and help you. I will hold you up with my victorious right hand. ISAIAH 41:10

☼ A prayer about SECURITY
When I'm standing on shaky ground

ETERNAL, ALL-POWERFUL GOD,

Regularly I seem to fall into the "snare of compare." As I measure myself against another mother, I find myself sorely lacking. I admit that I gravitate toward finding my security in accomplishments and the applause of others. All these futile pursuits leave me on shaky ground.

You are my rock, Lord. You are my secure and firm foundation. Let me hide myself daily in you. Guard my heart and mind by reminding me of your steadfast love. Thank you for being my Savior. Your grace is a safe sanctuary where I am free to express myself. Protect me, Lord, from trying to be someone I am not. You are a shield, protecting me from the fiery lies of the evil one. Your Word reminds me that you alone are the safest place for my identity to rest.

The LORD is my rock, my fortress, and my savior; my God is my rock, in whom I find protection. He is my shield, the power that saves me, and my place of safety. PSALM 18:2

⚙ A prayer about CREATIVITY
When I want to praise you for your wonders

CREATOR GOD,

Ah, what a glorious day to enjoy your creation. Thank you for giving us such a beautiful world in which to live this temporary life. I can only imagine what the next one holds. I pray that the wonders of your hand will continually point me to the wonders of your heart. Please awaken my children to your creativity as well.

O LORD, what a variety of things you have made! In wisdom you have made them all. PSALM 104:24

⚙ A prayer about COMPLAINING
When home becomes a dumping ground

GOD,

As a family, we need the freedom to be ourselves at home. But lately it seems we share our gripes more than our joys. Help us to practice gratitude instead of complaining, and let this mind-set begin with me. Let my family hear me making efforts to bless with my words. I pray that this new habit of thankfulness will be an infectious source of joy for all of us.

Let everything you say be good and helpful, so that your words will be an encouragement to those who hear them.
EPHESIANS 4:29

☀ **A prayer about PEACE**
When I need to be made whole

GOD,

I have returned home after a very long and hectic day when seemingly everyone and everything I encountered were in utter chaos. I am keenly aware that the disarray and confusion I am surrounded by is not the way you intended life to be from the beginning of time.

You, God, are the Creator who brings meaning, purpose, and life out of darkness. I long for you to make this a reality in my heart. I need to sense your peace that passes understanding. I long to have my fragmented and splintered life replaced by a wholeness that can come only from you. O Lord, please fill the void in my life with your joy and peace as I learn daily what it means to take you at your Word and trust that you have a plan and purpose for my life. Instead of my life overflowing with frustrations, despair, and tears, would you fill me up with an awareness of your love? I need a hope that does not disappoint or leave me aimless. God, I need to rely on your peace moment by moment.

I pray that God, the source of hope, will fill you completely with joy and peace because you trust in him. Then you will overflow with confident hope through the power of the Holy Spirit. ROMANS 15:13

⚙ **A prayer about GUIDANCE**
When I need help finding my way

HEAVENLY FATHER,

I wish there was a road map to life—something I could consult every day to make sure I'm on the right path. I want so badly to make the right choices in my parenting, and I sometimes feel as if I am losing my way. If I could see where my choices and decisions were taking me, it would make the journey so much clearer.

I forget that you have provided a road map for me in your Word and that you invite me to immerse myself in you. When I learn to truly abide, you will direct my path and walk with me along the journey. This takes intentional effort on my part, so show me how to remain in you and be with you daily. Remind me to spend time reading your road map for my life every day.

Remain in me, and I will remain in you. For a branch cannot produce fruit if it is severed from the vine, and you cannot be fruitful unless you remain in me. JOHN 15:4

DAY 143

☀ **A prayer about BURNOUT**
When I feel driven into the ground

LORD,

I need your lightness today. I'm worn out from pushing so hard, and I need another way to do things. On the one hand, I love my drive. It challenges me, excites me, keeps me dreaming, and never lets me stay bored. But lately that same sense of ambition has pushed me to a breaking point. I'm exhausted, and I need your help to strengthen me and help me find a better balance between work and rest.

And another thing, Lord. If there's any unhealthy motivation to my desire to succeed—whether it's the chance to build my own kingdom, to be seen as capable and worthwhile because of what I do, or to show up someone else—please cleanse me of those motives. I choose to rest in you now instead of wearing myself out trying to be someone special. Please guide my drive and use it to glorify yourself and to build your kingdom—in your time.

Jesus said, "Come to me, all of you who are weary and carry heavy burdens, and I will give you rest. Take my yoke upon you. Let me teach you, because I am humble and gentle at heart, and you will find rest for your souls. For my yoke is easy to bear, and the burden I give you is light."
MATTHEW 11:28-30

⚙ A prayer about ABSOLUTE TRUTH
When the world desires gray

GOD,

I'm not sure whether to turn off the TV in disgust or watch longer and pray harder. I want to know what's going on in the world, but my emotions run on a roller coaster when messages from the media dull your black-and-white truths into gray. God, most of the world doesn't want to hear about you, but you are exactly who we need. What is my role in standing up for truth? How do I show grace without compromising on the areas that lead people away from you? These questions never fail to draw deep sighs from me. Do you sigh often as you watch us on earth?

Please impress even more clearly on me the non-negotiable truths about yourself: Jesus is the only Savior; you are the only God worthy of worship; one day all will bow down to you; your love is everlasting; your gracious heart longs for each of us to receive and celebrate your forgiveness. Help me to proclaim your absolute truth while exhibiting your grace in all I say and do. And make that combination shocking in its appeal.

Jesus is . . . "The stone that you builders rejected [that] has now become the cornerstone." There is salvation in no one else! God has given no other name under heaven by which we must be saved. ACTS 4:11-12

☼ A prayer about STRENGTH
When I need a renewed perspective

HEAVENLY FATHER,

I am thankful for older and wiser parents I know who have encouraged me by letting me know that parenting is a marathon and not a sprint. Yet as I step on another small toy, I wonder how I will ever make it to the finish line. I wonder what roadblocks and hindrances I will encounter along the way. How will I endure when the race still ahead seems so long?

O Father, help me trust you with all the unseen and unknown aspects of this race. Through your Word and prayer, help me rise above the mundane and see the bigger picture. Your goal for my children is that they will eventually reach maturity in their faith-walk with you. Help them to discover how you have made them. Support them as they step out in faith to employ their gifts for your glory. God, please give me perspective and endurance for the long periods of time when I will see very little evidence of your work in their lives. Renew my strength today, and let me soar on high with you.

Those who trust in the LORD will find new strength. They will soar high on wings like eagles. They will run and not grow weary. They will walk and not faint. ISAIAH 40:31

☀ **A prayer about SATISFACTION**
  When I am left empty and unsatisfied

SAVIOR,

Certain insatiable appetites—whether for attention, praise, or even just caffeine—seem to rule my life. I hunger and thirst for things that will never satisfy. These temporal pursuits always leave me feeling empty and unfulfilled. Please give me a renewed appetite, Lord, a desire to zealously pursue you and your Word. Thank you for the assurance that as we chase after the things that please you, we will be blessed and satisfied.

God blesses those who hunger and thirst for justice, for they will be satisfied. MATTHEW 5:6

DAY 147 *Prayerful Moment*

☀ **A prayer about PAIN**
  When I need God's comfort

LORD,

You are my shelter and refuge from life's storms. Knowing that you see each tear that falls and promise never to leave me brings me such comfort. Thank you for being the Great Physician in the midst of my pain.

He will wipe every tear from their eyes, and there will be no more death or sorrow or crying or pain. All these things are gone forever. REVELATION 21:4

☼ A prayer about CIRCUMSTANCES
When I need to remember that God is bigger than my situation

HEAVENLY FATHER,

I feel as if I'm drowning under the pressure. I can't keep up, and my heart feels so heavy. Lord, you say that you're with me, that you're mighty to save. I don't feel your delight right now, but I'm counting on your love.

Will you please calm my heart as you work on my circumstances? I've heard that you either calm the storm or calm your child. I'll take either one, Lord. I just need fresh faith to believe your promises and trust your faithfulness. Sometimes I worry about being overtaken by my situation, and you seem so silent. Even if you choose to remain silent, I can trust you and rest in what I know about you—that you love me and are working plans for my best. Please grant me grace in all this to believe you. Thank you for singing over me right now.

For the LORD your God is living among you. He is a mighty savior. He will take delight in you with gladness. With his love, he will calm all your fears. He will rejoice over you with joyful songs. ZEPHANIAH 3:17

⚙ **A prayer about OBEDIENCE**
When I want to go my own way

LORD,

As I watched my child throw a full-blown tantrum recently, I realized that I can be just as childish when it comes to getting my way. While I may not physically throw my body to the ground and wail at the top of my lungs, I am sometimes just as defiant in telling you that I don't want to follow your will. I think my way is the best way, and I don't care to trust you with all of my decisions.

I want to learn to treat my own child with the same patience and love you show me when I am throwing my tantrums. You gently wait for me to finish my outburst and allow you to guide me—usually after I have fallen flat on my face. I don't know why I wait until I fail before relinquishing my tight hold on my life to you. I am sorry for not trusting you and letting you show me the right path. Transform my heart into one of humble obedience.

Samuel replied, "What is more pleasing to the LORD: your burnt offerings and sacrifices or your obedience to his voice? Listen! Obedience is better than sacrifice, and submission is better than offering the fat of rams." 1 SAMUEL 15:22

☼ **A prayer about ACCEPTANCE**
When I struggle with my child's actions

LORD,

You saw it too. We both watched my child act horribly.
This behavior pattern is becoming common, and quite
honestly, it's affecting my acceptance of him. That's hard
to admit. I would hate for him to sense my dissatisfaction
in him as a person. He is so much more than his actions,
but I struggle to keep that in mind when his selfish choices
seem to dominate his nature.

Heavenly Father, help me be the parent he needs. You
accept me, messed-up heart and all. Let your Spirit reign
in mine so that my loving boundaries speak volumes of
acceptance of his personhood while not letting him get
away with the wrong he keeps doing. This is a matter of
the heart for both my child and me, and what he sees in
my heart regarding him will impact him positively or negatively for the rest of his life. That's a weighty burden to
bear. But you are my perfect Parent, and I'm trusting you
to help me grow. Change my heart as it needs in order to
help heal and transform his. Thank you for modeling how
to love when it's tough.

May the words of my mouth and the meditation of my heart
be pleasing to you, O LORD, my rock and my redeemer.
PSALM 19:14

DAY 151

☼ **A prayer about FEELINGS**
When I am filled with misgivings and doubts

FATHER,

Every moment is the right time to trust you. But when my heart is fearful and uncertain, I want to run and hide. When I am angry, I want to try to gain some modicum of control. During the long days of despair, I feel vulnerable and exposed, longing for a safe place to rest.

So today, whether I experience a highest high or a lowest low, I am choosing to trust in you. I pour all my anxieties and needs at your feet. You have extended an open invitation for us to meet you at the throne of grace. When I am tempted to allow my feelings to rise and fall with the changes in my circumstances, please remind me that it's not about trying harder, but about trusting more completely. Forgive my doubts, my unspoken fear that you do not truly have my best interests at heart when unexpected events knock me down. You, Father, are my refuge and my rock. May I be planted firmly in the reality of your sovereign care.

O my people, trust in him at all times. Pour out your heart to him, for God is our refuge. PSALM 62:8

☀ **A prayer about UNITY**
When I have broken relationships

LORD JESUS,

All last words are precious, but especially yours as you set your face toward the Cross. These words challenge and convict me. You loved us enough to pray for us. You recognized that one of the greatest threats to us is brokenness in our relationships with you and others. Over the years you have underscored for me that the vital link to experiencing peace with others really lies in whether I am at peace with you and at peace within.

Forgive me for allowing conflict with others to exist. I know it grieves your heart and taints my witness to a watching world. The truth is that my unity with you and others will either validate or negate the claims of the gospel. Pursuing reconciliation and peace is not a casual matter. Help me to keep short accounts with you and others. I long to be a woman who is quick to repent. Help me to move today in love toward those whom I have offended. May I forgive others with the same lavish grace with which you have forgiven me.

I pray that they will all be one, just as you and I are one—as you are in me, Father, and I am in you. And may they be in us so that the world will believe you sent me. JOHN 17:21

☼ A prayer about PARENTING
  When I feel the weight of responsibility

LORD,

You have entrusted me with these little lives to nurture and protect. I am humbled by the task before me. Help me to show my children how to love you with all their heart, soul, and mind. Enable me to build them up so they can embrace their uniqueness and learn to use their talents and gifts for your glory.

Direct your children onto the right path, and when they are older, they will not leave it. PROVERBS 22:6

DAY 154 *Prayerful Moment*

☼ A prayer about BALANCE
  When you tell us to go against current trends

LORD,

You often move your true listeners along unusual paths. Please help my children learn to listen to you instead of blindly following trends. Help them balance the pull of outside pressure with the courage to step outside the norm at your instruction.

Don't copy the behavior and customs of this world, but let God transform you into a new person by changing the way you think. Then you will learn to know God's will for you, which is good and pleasing and perfect. ROMANS 12:2

☼ A prayer about the WILL OF GOD
When I want to seek your ultimate purpose for my life

FATHER,

When my children were young and disobeyed, they would try to hide from you and likely from me as well. They did not remember that you know whether we are in the center of your will and that you examine all our thoughts, actions, and motives. But I also often forget your sovereign gaze and try to cover my sin and shame with flimsy justifications.

My children have grown older and now live outside my purview but never outside yours. I pray for them today, that they would be seeking to put you first in their lives. May their primary pursuit be to live in the center of your ordained will. In that place we find purpose, satisfaction, and great joy. Give them wisdom and discernment as they make daily decisions. Please rekindle in them a love for your Word and give them the grace to live in orientation with its truths. May my children and I grow closer to each other as we pursue staying close to you.

Seek his will in all you do, and he will show you which path to take. PROVERBS 3:6

☼ A prayer about QUIETNESS
When I need rest

GOD,

I admit I am addicted to drama and commotion. Ironically, I find some comfort in the unpredictability that chaos can bring. Silence and ceasing from activity can sometimes scare me. God, I know that I need to return to you as my first love. Help me to rest from my labors and cares and to rest in you. Comfort me with your sovereign care and provision. I confess I am weary of trying to do life in my own strength.

Lord, I want to trust in you and your plan for me. As a mother I need confidence to fulfill this calling. Help me see that it can only be acquired by quieting my heart and soul before you. God, I surrender to the silence and will seek to accept the rest, quietness, and confidence offered in and through Jesus Christ.

This is what the Sovereign LORD, the Holy One of Israel, says: "Only in returning to me and resting in me will you be saved. In quietness and confidence is your strength."
ISAIAH 30:15

☼ A prayer about the POWER OF GOD
When I need to know just how powerless I am

GOD,

Whatever made me think I had the power to control anything? Yet I still wake up each day thinking that I can actually cause things to happen. Often I run after this notion until I come to the end of my strength, my ideas, and myself. God, is this the only way for me to truly understand that you are the reference point for every part of my life?

Everything that exists in my world comes from your good hand, and I am so thankful that everything you give you also sustain. Forgive me for my tiny efforts to try to maintain *any* aspect of my life. I thank you that as you provide and support all things, you always have a purpose greater than the ones I think I can see. You alone, God, have the power to cause all things to work together for the glory of your name.

Everything comes from him and exists by his power and is intended for his glory. All glory to him forever! Amen.
ROMANS 11:36

☼ A prayer about KINDNESS
When I want revenge

O LORD,

There are few things worse than when someone hurts my child. The raging mother bear inside of me is awakened and I want to come out fighting. And while there are times when you do ask me to protect or stand up for my child, more often you direct me to repay the wrong with compassion. It is not natural for me to want to be kind to my (or my child's) enemies, and I can't do it in my own strength.

I need you to give me the power to hold my tongue. I need your words to teach my child to learn when to turn the other cheek and when to stand up for herself. Remind me that you can use our kindness in the face of wrongdoing to bring others to you. And remind us that you have shown us kindness when we don't deserve it.

Love your enemies! Do good to them. Lend to them without expecting to be repaid. Then your reward from heaven will be very great, and you will truly be acting as children of the Most High, for he is kind to those who are unthankful and wicked. LUKE 6:35

⚜ **A prayer about CULTURE**
When I want to make a positive impact

GOD,

There has to be more. Yes, this world is still headed for destruction. Yes, our default is to let our human nature lead, even when we've heard you say your way is far better. But I'm weary of just complaining about the troubles, of worrying about how my children will be affected by the faulty logic, the "truths" they're taught that sound so good on the surface.

Lord, I want to raise them not just to avoid the negatives but to be strong influencers for your way. You did not call us only to be on the defensive about our faith. Yes, it is vital to know what we believe and why, and to have the courage to stand up for your truth. But we also must know how to share that truth in a loving, healing way that draws people to your holiness. Lord, build into my children (and me) the unshakable faith that believes you move mountains and the assurance that you desire us to help you. May these young souls in my care impact our culture for you.

While Paul was waiting for them in Athens, he was deeply troubled by all the idols he saw everywhere in the city. He went to the synagogue to reason with the Jews and the God-fearing Gentiles, and he spoke daily in the public square to all who happened to be there. ACTS 17:16-17

☼ A prayer about TRUST
When I need a better plan for my life

LORD,

You know all about my tendency to rely on my own plans and patterns. For far too long I have leaned on my own understanding and experiences. Yet I find no lasting peace and contentment on my own. So even though my heart is filled with fear of the unknown, I submit myself to your sovereign plan today. I rest in the security of your providential blueprint for my life.

Trust in the LORD with all your heart; do not depend on your own understanding. PROVERBS 3:5

☼ A prayer about TOUCH
When I need a tender moment

LORD,

As I nurse my youngest, I thank you for these quiet, intimate opportunities to bond with my baby. The peace and security of this moment reassure me. The closeness I feel with this child is a dim reflection of the bond you and I share. Thank you for drawing near to me and bringing me close to your heart. Your oversight of my life nourishes and protects me. May I always rest in your everlasting arms.

I have calmed and quieted myself, like a weaned child who no longer cries for its mother's milk. Yes, like a weaned child is my soul within me. PSALM 131:2

☼ A prayer about REPENTANCE
When I need my heart to be broken

HEAVENLY FATHER,

You search my heart and see into the deepest, darkest corners of my thoughts and intentions. The sin within me is breaking my heart, but I need to remember that it breaks your heart even more. Lord, I am blind to many of my inadequacies and shortcomings. Will you graciously show me areas of my heart that have been unexamined far too long? As you reveal my dreadful ways, please give me a godly sorrow over these areas.

Lord, I take great comfort in the fact that as I bring you my sin, you offer the free gift of forgiveness. You will not reject the offerings of a repentant heart. I treasure the Cross and all that your blood has accomplished on my behalf. Help me not to remain in my sorrow but to move forward in faith, believing that you have fully washed away my sins and stand faithful to guide me in paths of righteousness.

The sacrifice you desire is a broken spirit. You will not reject a broken and repentant heart, O God. PSALM 51:17

☀ A prayer about REDEMPTION
When I need to be reclaimed

LORD,

My purse is overflowing with coupons and offers that sometimes seem too good to be true. I ponder for a moment if I should redeem some of these things today or let them sit another day, waiting to be cashed out. I am struck for a moment by how I am enticed by these offers, although most of them are for fleeting pleasures such as food and material goods.

The potential for the transfer of goods in my pocketbook points to a greater truth that I need to be reminded of today: I have been bought with a much higher price than buy-one-get-one-free. I have been redeemed—not for something temporal that will fade away, but rather for a place that is eternal and filled with joy forever. Thank you, Lord, for meeting me in my suffering and rescuing me so often from vain pursuits. You have sought me with love and mercy. You have lifted, carried, and sustained me all the days of my life.

In all their suffering he also suffered, and he personally rescued them. In his love and mercy he redeemed them. He lifted them up and carried them through all the years.
ISAIAH 63:9

☼ A prayer about GRIEF
When I need comfort

LORD,

I am overwhelmed with sadness. In a heartbeat, someone I love was snatched away from me. Now I am completely bereft. One moment I am numb; the next I am angry. I feel as if I am stumbling through life. Although I know you are walking with me and haven't left me alone, I am having trouble feeling your presence in the midst of the darkness.

Remind me again that you are right here with me, cradling me in your ever-loving arms. You mourn right along with me and see every tear that falls. Be present with me and carry me through the pain. Let your love wash over me in a tangible way so I can feel your presence in my darkest hour. Thank you for never abandoning me and for loving me in the midst of tragedy.

I waited patiently for the LORD to help me, and he turned to me and heard my cry. He lifted me out of the pit of despair, out of the mud and the mire. He set my feet on solid ground and steadied me as I walked along. PSALM 40:1-2

⚙ **A prayer about LOYALTY**
When I get discouraged

HEAVENLY FATHER,

Integrity seems to be a dying virtue in our culture today. Every day it seems I hear of another cheating scandal in the news and another broken marriage in my community. My heart breaks for those who have been hurt by the thoughtless actions of others. It seems that no one values putting others first or sticking by each other through the hard times when it is so much easier to move on to the next relationship.

In a world full of brokenness, your faithfulness is the example I want to follow in my relationships. You have kept your promises, and you show me that it is possible to make lasting commitments. Help me to model this value to my children the way you have modeled it to me. Then grant them the desire and the strength to remain loyal to their siblings, their friends, and most of all to you, O Lord.

Never let loyalty and kindness leave you! Tie them around your neck as a reminder. Write them deep within your heart.
PROVERBS 3:3

☼ A prayer about FORGIVENESS
When I need to let go of hurts

LORD,

I spend far too much of my time holding on to the wrongs that have been done to me. My kids have hurt my feelings, disobeyed me, or sinned against me; my family members have wronged me; my friends have forsaken me; and the list goes on and on. I could spend all of my time cataloging the things that others have done to make me angry, sad, or disillusioned.

But you have asked me to be a forgiver—even when I don't feel it is deserved. I am unable to do this in my own strength today. Please give me your grace and forgiveness toward those who have hurt me. Help me to give those slights and frustrations entirely into your hands so that I don't hang on to them any longer. Thank you for being the model of mercy in my own life. Thank you for pardoning me time and again when I have sinned against you. Mold my heart to be more like yours today.

He is so rich in kindness and grace that he purchased our freedom with the blood of his Son and forgave our sins.
EPHESIANS 1:7

☼ A prayer about GRACE
When I need perspective

O FATHER,

My child can drive me crazy. Why can't he just listen and obey? When I get so annoyed that I'm tempted to ream him out, please put a check on my spirit. Remind me of the grace you have extended to me. Help me to see how hypocritical it would be for me not to extend this same grace to my child. Fill me with your grace and forgiveness. They don't come naturally to me.

Let us come boldly to the throne of our gracious God. There we will receive his mercy, and we will find grace to help us when we need it most. HEBREWS 4:16

DAY 168 *Prayerful Moment*

☼ A prayer about CONTENTMENT
When I wonder how satisfaction happens

FATHER,

Though I struggle with feeling content, I want to thank you for knowing the path to true, unshakable fulfillment. What a mystery to my human heart! The apostle Paul learned to be content through seeking you first in every struggle he faced. Maybe the gaping hole of want is the key to real satisfaction if it drives me deeper with you. Is that how it happens, Lord? If so, then meet me in this aching desire.

I have learned how to be content with whatever I have.
PHILIPPIANS 4:11

☀ **A prayer about TRUTH**
When I treat your Word far too casually

GOD,

We live in a world where finding the value of truth is like searching for a treasure in shifting sands. My children are being bombarded by worldviews that are antithetical and often hostile to you. Increasingly, they are paying a price for standing up for what they believe. I confess that some days I have been far too casual in imparting truth to my kids. I fall into the trap of believing that instruction in godly living is to be relegated to Sundays or to other individuals in the church.

As we journey through life together, help me realize that every moment is a unique opportunity to see your truth in a fresh and relevant way. Show me areas of my life where I have forsaken truth to believe in lies. I know that by failing to take those lies captive and then destroy them, I will impact my children for ill rather than for their good. Give our family bravery to stand for truth even when it is unpopular or countercultural. May your truth transform our minds, hearts, and home.

You must commit yourselves wholeheartedly to these commands that I am giving you today.
DEUTERONOMY 6:6

☼ A prayer about DECEPTION
When I see my kids wonder whom to believe

FATHER,

You see even more than I can how many temptations my kids face daily. As mistruths from society bombard them, plant your truths in their minds. Bathe their hearts with your Spirit, and give them discernment to recognize when something that sounds good really is not.

No matter how old they grow, they will be susceptible to following after beliefs that don't honor you or edify them. Warn them of pitfalls ahead, and help them steer clear of those first missteps that lead them into being fooled by something that is not of you. Give them shrewdness to stand up for truth with firm and gentle honesty. And Lord, help me to live honorably so they can respect the reasons why I choose to live in your truth.

Satan disguises himself as an angel of light. So it is no wonder that his servants also disguise themselves as servants of righteousness. In the end they will get the punishment their wicked deeds deserve. 2 CORINTHIANS 11:14-15

☼ A prayer about LIFE'S DEMANDS
When I feel overwhelmed

LORD JESUS,

There are piles of laundry on the floor, dirty dishes in the sink, kids who need homework help, bills to pay, and e-mails to answer. The to-do list never seems to get shorter, and I always feel behind. The easiest thing to give up is my quiet time, but that is what I need the most. Time spent with you is never wasted, and I always feel rejuvenated after I sit with you for a while. You fill my soul and renew my energy.

Don't let me push you aside today. Pursue me. Remind me once again that you desire to carry my burdens and provide a respite in this busy season. Prioritize my to-do list for me so I am following your will. Help me to say no when necessary to free me up to follow you. Thank you for being patient with me when I forget to turn to you.

Those who trust in the LORD will find new strength. They will soar high on wings like eagles. They will run and not grow weary. They will walk and not faint.
ISAIAH 40:31

☼ A prayer about HELPING
When I want to be used by God

GOD,

In the beginning, in all of creation, only one thing was not good—for Adam to be alone. As I have traveled lately, I have become keenly aware that it is also not good for my marriage or my family to be left without my help. Give me grace to be a helper to my family and not a hinderer. I want to come alongside my husband as he graciously leads our family. Give me insight to anticipate how I can provide for our children's needs and desires. I want to model for my children your mission to serve and not to be served.

You, God, are the reference point for what being a helper means. Over the years you have comforted me, provided for me, and supplied all my needs. I aspire for our family to work in harmony in such a way that glorifies you. Help me to rely on your strength and please give me wisdom to support and encourage those whom I love so dearly.

The LORD God said, "It is not good for the man to be alone. I will make a helper who is just right for him."

GENESIS 2:18

☀ A prayer about ANGER
When I feel mine simmering

LORD,

Will these kids ever learn? They did it again—because they are kids. And I did it again, too, because I am still in need of your fine-tuning: I crossed the line to that angry place where I react with hostility instead of tempering my response with grace. Will *I* ever learn?

My children will continue to do things that frustrate me, and my patience will not only be tested, it will *feel* tested. I will feel angry at times. Thank you for not condemning me for that.

But Lord, I felt my anger take over again, and that's got to change. I can't love like you do when anger is in charge. And I can't realign my heart with lasting results, but you can. Please clean out this seed of rage in me so I don't give the enemy an opportunity to develop something unwholesome in my children or myself. Thank you for not raging at me. May your gracious character in my life show my children how to respond well despite frustrations.

"Don't sin by letting anger control you." Don't let the sun go down while you are still angry, for anger gives a foothold to the devil. EPHESIANS 4:26-27

☼ A prayer about BUSYNESS
When to-dos threaten wiser living

LORD,

I'm too busy and it shows. When tasks take over, I frequently put off my family with excuses of "I don't have time" or "I'm too busy." Lord, slow me down so I don't unwisely make my kids grow up feeling like interruptions. The time for the wisest priorities is now.

Be careful how you live. Don't live like fools, but like those who are wise. Make the most of every opportunity. . . . Don't act thoughtlessly, but understand what the Lord wants you to do. EPHESIANS 5:15-17

☼ A prayer about OVERCOMING
When I need victory over sins

FATHER,

I come to you in distress, suffering from the effects of repeated sins in my life. I am in bondage to this cycle of offense against you. I come now humbly in prayer, asking you to deliver me. Set me free from these shackles and help me to walk in liberty.

In my distress I prayed to the LORD, and the LORD answered me and set me free. PSALM 118:5

☀ **A prayer about STRESS**
When I need to trust God for my provisions

GOD ABOVE,

I am finding it difficult indeed to rejoice over our current financial trials. I awake each morning wondering how you will provide all that we need. I go to sleep at night wondering how I could possibly have anticipated so many unexpected expenditures. I know my joy cannot be rooted in my circumstances. I have allowed my emotions to race up and down as quickly as my situations have changed.

You have promised that you will always provide daily bread. Yet I am constantly trying to borrow grace for another day and my potential future needs. Settle my soul and increase my dependence on you. You have provided for your children since the beginning of creation. Forgive my doubts and unfounded fears. I recognize that walking through this journey of learning to trust you has far more to do with my spiritual formation than anything else. I am confident that you love me and will never leave or forsake me. Please give me endurance and faith to believe you have a magnificent plan for my family. Thank you, God, for always watching over every detail of our lives.

We can rejoice, too, when we run into problems and trials, for we know that they help us develop endurance.
ROMANS 5:3

☀ A prayer about WORSHIP
When I am drawn to put things in God's place

ALMIGHTY GOD,

Forgive my wandering heart that is easily enticed by insignificant matters. You are a jealous God and will not abide divided worship. Many things and relationships in my life are good or even great, but I elevate them way beyond their worth. I even act as though my children, my home, or my friendships are of ultimate value. When my heart is enamored with serving and promoting these more than you, I have become an idolater.

Worship belongs to you alone. You are holy, perfect, honorable, and worthy of all my praise. I repent of ascribing worth to what is worthless. I have wasted more time and resources than I care to admit. Please continue your sanctifying work in me until my devotion to you is exclusive.

You must not bow down to them or worship them, for I, the LORD your God, am a jealous God who will not tolerate your affection for any other gods. I lay the sins of the parents upon their children; the entire family is affected—even children in the third and fourth generations of those who reject me. EXODUS 20:5

☼ A prayer about ENTHUSIASM
When I want to enjoy your Spirit . . . quietly

LORD,

I am so thankful that enthusiasm can be quiet. Usually I think of it as cheering, jumping up and down, and approaching every task and conversation with a radiant smile. You know me better than that, God. Sometimes I don't have a smile ready to pull out at a moment's notice. It certainly doesn't stay plastered on my face every second.

Thank you that enthusiasm involves simply revealing through my countenance that you are within me. "God in me." That's what the word *enthusiasm* means, and since quite often you show yourself to me in gentle ways, I can point others to your presence just as gently and peacefully. You don't need loud fanfare, though you deserve it. In fact, sometimes the greatest gifts leave us speechless, so right now I offer you my quiet, enthusiastic worship. Lord, when it's time for me to share you verbally and with a big smile, please let those things flow from me. Otherwise, I pray that your sweet Spirit would stream consistently from my daily life.

Give your bodies to God because of all he has done for you. Let them be a living and holy sacrifice—the kind he will find acceptable. This is truly the way to worship him.
ROMANS 12:1

☼ A prayer about SELF-CONTROL
When I need to restrain myself

HOLY SPIRIT,

Today, as I was busy in another room, I heard my children fighting. They sounded out of control, and I am beginning to feel the same way. Spirit, you are so patient with your own children, including me. Please teach me how to treat my children that way. I know self-control is a fruit that is produced as you dwell in us. Fill my children and me today with a full portion of yourself. I know that when we fail to exercise self-control, we leave ourselves vulnerable to attacks from Satan. We can be tempted to be passive when it comes to trying to control our selfish desires.

Spirit, incline our hearts to submit our self-centered desires to your sovereign control. Change our hearts to put others first and consider their needs as more important than our own. Bring harmony and peace to our family as we try relating to one another with grace and loyalty.

A person without self-control is like a city with broken-down walls. PROVERBS 25:28

☀ A prayer about my child's HEART
When I think of my child's future

GOD,

The world is a harsh and scary place, and I want to shelter and protect my child from anything that has potential to harm her. I can get caught up in ruminating on all the potential dangers that lurk behind every door. I know that trying to shelter my child too much is ultimately not in her best interest. It doesn't help her learn and grow. But my fear gets in the way and threatens to overtake me.

I give you my child's heart today, Lord. I trust you to protect her and walk with her through any trials and struggles that come her way. Thank you for loving my child even more than I do. Soften her heart so she grows to love you and trust you with her life. Strengthen her mind so that she may become a wise and discerning woman.

I could have no greater joy than to hear that my children are following the truth. 3 JOHN 1:4

❋ A prayer about CONTENTMENT
When I struggle with dissatisfaction

LORD,

I slipped up again. Whenever this unproductive desire rises in me, I know I'm helped by focusing more on you. Sometimes I wonder if this chronic struggle is your unique method of mercy to draw me closer to yourself. Thank you that when I soak up your Word and linger with you, you never leave me unsatisfied. In fact, you fulfill my deepest unmet longings and desires.

Seek the Kingdom of God above all else, and live righteously, and he will give you everything you need. MATTHEW 6:33

DAY 182 *Prayerful Moment*

❋ A prayer about WORSHIP
When I need to keep the main thing the main thing

FATHER,

I am often distracted by small matters and make them much larger than they deserve. Help me remember that eventually every knee will bow and every tongue will confess your greatness. Every wrong will be made right, and every broken relationship will be restored. Let me live in the security of knowing that you will be victorious in the end.

Who will not fear you, Lord, and glorify your name? For you alone are holy. All nations will come and worship before you, for your righteous deeds have been revealed.
REVELATION 15:4

☼ A prayer about REST
When I want to escape

GOD,

I want to escape from all the noise and clamor. Oh, that I could fly away to a peaceful and serene place. I yearn for freedom from anxiety and cares. I desire to escape the drudgery of my days and relax. I know, Lord, that every day brings troubles of its own, but what really counts is my reaction to those issues and concerns. My heart needs peace with you and peace within. Please grant me a more settled and secure heart, one that is steady, consistent, and growing in my trust in your plan for my life.

Father, I am tired of running rather than resting. Perhaps I can rest as I run in *your* power and strength. Because my relationship with you is fixed and immovable, I can rest in the fact that you will never fail to provide for my every need. God, if I could fly anywhere, it would be to the eventual rest that will come on the final day.

Oh, that I had wings like a dove; then I would fly away and rest! PSALM 55:6

⚜ A prayer about LISTENING
When I need to tune in to God's voice

O LORD,

The noise of the world so easily creeps into my mind and pushes you out. I am distracted by the chatter of others' needs and wants—not to mention my own. My days are filled with all the things I should do in order to be a good mother, a good worker, a good Christian. All of these are appropriate in and of themselves—but I can become so consumed with them that I forget to stop and listen for you and your guidance. I don't know how to strike the balance between doing good and listening for your voice.

So I ask you to show me. Help me to take the time to cease my doing and just be in your presence. Thank you for promising to always show up when I do listen to you. Speak, Lord, I am listening.

Be still, and know that I am God! I will be honored by every nation. I will be honored throughout the world.
PSALM 46:10

✻ A prayer about HEAVEN
When I am discouraged

JESUS,

I am so grateful for the life you have given me. You have heaped blessings on me so numerous I can't even begin to count them. Each day I am able to spend with my child is a gift. You have brought people into my life to give me counsel, support, and admonition. I am truly grateful for your many gifts. I'm overwhelmed when I consider that you have promised me so much more in heaven. I can't fathom what it will be like to live in your presence every day in a place without pain or suffering. I do long for the day when I am with you in paradise.

But right now, you have me right where I am for a reason. Help me to fulfill my purpose while I am here and use every minute for your glory. Help me not to get discouraged, but to hold on to your promises when things get difficult. Thank you for going ahead of me to prepare a place for me in heaven.

To me, living means living for Christ, and dying is even better. But if I live, I can do more fruitful work for Christ. So I really don't know which is better. I'm torn between two desires: I long to go and be with Christ, which would be far better for me. PHILIPPIANS 1:21-23

☼ A prayer about HEALTH
When my child is hurting

LORD,

It is so hard to watch my child suffer. I just want to fix her problem and take away the pain. I feel so helpless. It would be so much easier if I were the one feeling this way. I would take this away in an instant if I could, but I am powerless in this situation.

I need you to take away the pain and walk with us through this. It is too hard to carry alone. Reach down and bring comfort to my child. Let her know that you are there and that you alone have the power to heal. Be with me as I suffer alongside her, and remind me that you love my child even more than I do. Help me to lean on you during this difficult time. Please bring your healing touch to both of us today.

When Jesus arrived at Peter's house, Peter's mother-in-law was sick in bed with a high fever. But when Jesus touched her hand, the fever left her. Then she got up and prepared a meal for him. That evening many demon-possessed people were brought to Jesus. He cast out the evil spirits with a simple command, and he healed all the sick. This fulfilled the word of the Lord through the prophet Isaiah, who said, "He took our sicknesses and removed our diseases."

MATTHEW 8:14-17

☼ A prayer about MOTIVATION
When I find myself doing things for the wrong reasons

HEAVENLY FATHER,

I am ashamed to admit that all too frequently I find myself doing things to please others rather than you. I want to impress. I want to do better than the other mothers. I want to have better-behaved children, a cleaner house, a fancier car . . . the list goes on and on. I spend so much time worrying about outward appearances and worldly pursuits that I do not focus on you and your pathway for me. I think deep down I am afraid that your plan doesn't include all of the things I think I need.

Help me to examine my motivation each day and align my thoughts and actions according to your will, not the will of the jealous monster inside of me. Help me to trust the plan you have for my life and to seek to live in your will each day.

"For I know the plans I have for you," says the LORD. "They are plans for good and not for disaster, to give you a future and a hope." JEREMIAH 29:11

☼ **A prayer about JOY**
When I need to celebrate

LORD,

Nothing is quite like watching children dance with exuberance. Their innocent pleasure at the smallest delights touches me and reminds me that I need to experience more joy in my life. Help me take the time to stop and be grateful for blessings you have given me. Help me to experience the joy that only you can bring.

The LORD is my strength and shield. I trust him with all my heart. He helps me, and my heart is filled with joy. I burst out in songs of thanksgiving. PSALM 28:7

DAY 189 *Prayerful Moment*

☼ **A prayer about RENEWAL**
When I long for a brighter tomorrow

LORD JESUS,

You know what I am thankful for today? Despite the hurts and disappointments in this life, I have your promise that one day tears, pain, and suffering will be no more. Even though life seems chaotic and unruly right now, you are still on the throne. You are making all things new. Thank you!

The one sitting on the throne said, "Look, I am making everything new!" And then he said to me, "Write this down, for what I tell you is trustworthy and true."
REVELATION 21:5

☀ A prayer about PATIENCE
When little things get on my nerves

LORD,

I hate to admit it, but petty matters have been bringing me down lately. Whether it is not finding a parking space when I am running late, having to stand in long lines at the grocery store, or dealing with a child who refuses to take a much-needed nap, I sometimes find my patience wearing thin. When I become impatient, it is easy for me to think of myself as a victim. The world seems to be against me, and I start complaining. This is not only an unproductive way to think, it is displeasing to you.

A more productive response would be to come to you and share my frustrations so that you can reframe my thoughts. You can turn them around and give me much-needed perspective. You can carry my burdens for me and provide me with rest so that I can respond more appropriately to things that are not going my way. Cultivate the fruit of patience in my heart today. Weed out any selfishness that has taken root and replace it with kindness and gentleness.

May God, who gives this patience and encouragement, help you live in complete harmony with each other, as is fitting for followers of Christ Jesus. ROMANS 15:5

☼ A prayer about PURPOSE
When I wonder why this is happening

GOD,

My mind and heart are swirling with questions about why you are allowing such pain and trials in my life. I know you love me and have an eternal purpose that you are achieving through this journey. I know this not because my circumstances are necessarily changing but because over the years you have helped me to know you and your character. I understand that you are using all things to refine me— the highs and the lows, the joy-filled moments and the sorrowful moments, the periods of suffering and the offerings of comfort.

God, I know that you are the master architect of my life and that each test you are allowing is conforming me more and more to your image. I long to live according to your divine purpose for my life. When my life is properly aligned with your ultimate purposes, I will find joy, security, and your unconditional love.

God causes everything to work together for the good of those who love God and are called according to his purpose for them. ROMANS 8:28

☀ A prayer about COURAGE
When bravery brings loss

FATHER,

It hurts to suffer for doing what's right, a lesson my child is learning. I've watched him pick himself up after friends have cast him off because he chose to live for you. I've heard him choke back tears when he didn't know I was within earshot. I've been hurting to see him lose for following you.

I wouldn't want him to choose any differently, but I do want him to experience your strength in tough times. Please comfort his heart and help him hold on to your promise to be with him and provide for his needs. Build his courage even more, and raise up friends to support him. When he feels alone, help us as his family to fill in the gaps and support him as well. Help us build up his courage and be a safety net of affirmation for who he is. Though the lesson is difficult and the losses are painful, reward him for living courageously for you rather than for people.

Work willingly at whatever you do, as though you were working for the Lord rather than for people. Remember that the Lord will give you an inheritance as your reward, and that the Master you are serving is Christ.
COLOSSIANS 3:23-24

☀ **A prayer about MEMORIES**
When I find the days flying by

LORD,

The days, which used to seem so long, are rushing by way too fast. I feel as if I'm watching my children grow from tiny babies to grown adults in an instant. My time with my children is so short; I want to be intentional about making memories with them that will last for eternity.

Help me to take advantage of stolen moments to talk and laugh with them. Teach me to let go of the things that don't matter so I can focus on building into my children a love for you, a heart for others, and a passion for the lost. Order my days so that I don't look back with regrets of time wasted and words thoughtlessly spoken. This time is a gift from you. Help me to spend each day with open eyes and a grateful heart.

For everything there is a season, a time for every activity under heaven. . . . Yet God has made everything beautiful for its own time. He has planted eternity in the human heart, but even so, people cannot see the whole scope of God's work from beginning to end.

ECCLESIASTES 3:1, 11

☀ A prayer about CHRISTLIKENESS
When I struggle to stay connected to you

LORD,

It never fails. The quality of my connection with you truly impacts my relationships with others and my contentment in daily tasks. On days when I feel as if everything I touch is destined for failure and I can't seem to coordinate the goals of my heart with the tasks at hand, I can trace the frustrations back to not spending time soaking up your Spirit.

Not only do I need your stabilizing presence, but my family needs me to stay close to you so that they can benefit from Christlikeness flowing out of me. When I rely on my own power and patience, eventually my human nature reveals itself. Please, Lord, nudge me gently and firmly to breathe you in and breathe out all the negatives before they do harm. Through you I can be a source of healing and joy for my family.

[Jesus said,] "Yes, I am the vine; you are the branches. Those who remain in me, and I in them, will produce much fruit. For apart from me you can do nothing." JOHN 15:5

☀ **A prayer about GENTLENESS**
   When I need to remember God's grace

LORD JESUS,

Cradling my baby in my arms late at night, I am struck anew by the grace and gentleness you show me every day. You lead me like a shepherd, gently guiding me back to the right path when I stray. Thank you for treating my heart with care.

He will feed his flock like a shepherd. He will carry the lambs in his arms, holding them close to his heart. He will gently lead the mother sheep with their young.
ISAIAH 40:11

☀ **A prayer about COMMUNICATION**
   When my kids and I don't understand each other

LORD,

My children and I are not communicating well. It's as if my words are bouncing senselessly against their ears and returning, unheeded, right back to me. We need your help to understand one another. Open our hearts so that we can work through our differences. Help us communicate effectively and patiently.

We have spoken honestly with you, and our hearts are open to you. . . . I am asking you to respond as if you were my own children. Open your hearts to us!
2 CORINTHIANS 6:11-13

※ **A prayer about RESPECT**
When I forget who is ultimately in charge

GOD,

Right now I am so angry because of the disrespectful behavior of my child. She has acted rudely and treated my husband and me so poorly. I have much that I would like to say to her, so please give me grace to pause and pray. Why did she say those things? What caused her to feel the freedom to raise her voice to us? What is going on in her heart and mind right now?

Lord, I fall short every day in pleasing you in my words and interactions with my children. Yes, I am stung by the disrespectful behavior from my child, but I wonder how often I have grieved your heart by my own disrespectful behavior. I know surrender and submission are necessary to relate rightly to you and to one another. Open my hands and my heart toward pursuing peace with my child and with you. Forgive me for reacting rather than resting in your best design for the relationships in my life.

Since we respected our earthly fathers who disciplined us, shouldn't we submit even more to the discipline of the Father of our spirits, and live forever?
HEBREWS 12:9

⚙ A prayer about HEAVEN
When I am reminded of God's ultimate promise

HEAVENLY FATHER,

Snuggling a freshly bathed baby is as close to heaven as I can imagine. I love feeling the soft baby skin against my cheek and the downy head burrowing into my neck. You have given me this precious baby as a reminder of your eternal love for me. I long for the day when I can leave this world behind me and live in perfect community with you.

Help me to keep my eyes focused on heaven today as I mother my child and go about my daily tasks. Remind me that the smallest act of kindness done out of love for you is more significant than the greatest achievement done to impress others. Fix my mind on the treasures you have stored up for me in heaven. And give me compassion for those who do not yet know you so that I might be inspired to share your love with them.

What we suffer now is nothing compared to the glory he will reveal to us later. ROMANS 8:18

⚙ **A prayer about feeling OVERWHELMED**
When there is too much to handle

LORD,

Today I am feeling bombarded on all fronts. I don't think I can mentally or physically handle everything I need to get done and the issues I need to resolve. I feel like yelling at everyone to just give me one minute to myself. I am having trouble tapping into your strength and displaying the fruit of your Spirit.

Help me to step back and find just a moment of peace so that I can rejuvenate my heart. Remove this self-imposed burden of feeling like I need to accomplish everything. Remind me of what is truly important. Give me the strength to get through today and start tomorrow with fresh perspective and renewed energy. And most important, fill me with your Spirit and help me to show your love to everyone around me despite my own personal stress.

The faithful love of the LORD never ends! His mercies never cease. Great is his faithfulness; his mercies begin afresh each morning. LAMENTATIONS 3:22-23

☼ A prayer about APPROVAL
When I feel the need to please others

GOD,

Is it obvious that I'm living by your standards, not to please the world? Many times I wonder if others can see my mind scramble to come up with a response I think they would approve of. Oftentimes I feel awful because I can tell I'm trying to be what someone else wants me to be. But you clarify things. Your approval is what counts, and if I'm seeking you and relying on your help to emulate your character, then you are pleased with me. Why do I find it so hard to receive your acceptance? Why can't I let my heart rest when I'm with others, since I don't need to question my worth? I have your approval. Period.

Please burn into me the desire for your approval above all others' and the gumption to let disapproving feedback roll off my soul when it is not from you. I can have complete peace if I rest in your approval. I only need to seek you first and fully. Thank you for your approval and the freedom you want me to relish.

Obviously, I'm not trying to win the approval of people, but of God. If pleasing people were my goal, I would not be Christ's servant. GALATIANS 1:10

☼ A prayer about PARENTING
When mothering seems smothering

LORD,

I confess that sometimes my kids' needs and wants are so overwhelming that I find I am losing myself. I miss the person I used to be—free with no pressures or responsibilities. Then I remember the joy I feel when I look at my sleeping child, so innocent and peaceful, and I am reminded of the great blessing it is to be a parent.

Help me to hold on to that feeling of joy and peace as I go through the day. Thank you for giving me this precious child, whom you love exponentially more than I can even imagine. Thank you for being my loving Father and for putting up with my frustration and doubts. Remind me once again of the growth and positive changes I've experienced since becoming a parent. Help me continue to grow and mature in my faith and my parenting today.

By his divine power, God has given us everything we need for living a godly life. We have received all of this by coming to know him, the one who called us to himself by means of his marvelous glory and excellence. 2 PETER 1:3

⚙ A prayer about APPEARANCE
When I focus too much on my physical shortcomings

CREATOR GOD,

Please help me to remember that my children notice what I focus on, including my sighs and derogatory comments about how I look. Please help my words, expressions, and habits reflect the respect I have for myself because I am made in your beautiful image. Help them learn to respect their own and others' innate beauty, which reflects you.

Then God said, "Let us make human beings in our image, to be like us." GENESIS 1:26

DAY 203 *Prayerful Moment*

⚙ A prayer about ENCOURAGEMENT
When my mood distracts me from offering hope

LORD,

Thank you for the reminder that all my interactions either offer hope and encouragement or miss the chance to do so. When my mood is low, please fill me with your grace. I don't want to miss the opportunity to act as your merciful, thoughtful daughter and make a positive difference in someone else's life.

Let's not get tired of doing what is good. At just the right time we will reap a harvest of blessing if we don't give up. GALATIANS 6:9

☼ A prayer about COMPASSION
When my concern for others runs low

FATHER,

You know that my heart can be big, that it tugs when someone is hurting. I do care.

But sometimes I struggle to show my care. For whatever reason—whether I feel drained or my schedule is especially full or someone's pain triggers pain for me—I feel my compassion pull inward. My heart feels small, and my response isn't what I think you want from me.

I feel guilty about this failure. Sometimes. Other times I feel impatience about whether I'm overanalyzing. Sometimes I just don't feel it in me to care right then because caring involves investments of time and emotions that I feel depleted of already. Lord, make my heart bigger. Please plant your kind of compassion in me—the kind that invests more time and fights more bravely—and help me to find rest in you. You promise to fill me when I'm doing what I can to fill others. Please help me grow in showing compassion.

Don't just pretend to love others. Really love them. Hate what is wrong. Hold tightly to what is good. Love each other with genuine affection, and take delight in honoring each other. ROMANS 12:9-10

☀ **A prayer about ABANDONMENT**
When I feel lonely and unworthy

GOD,

How many people will spend today feeling lonely? Forgotten? Overlooked? Abandoned? I'm guessing lots. I ask because I know you see the exact number, but I'm not sure my heart could handle knowing how much pain this earth experiences. It takes only a taste of heartache to understand some of the agony of being alone in life. I understand that. Loneliness can reduce my heart to believing a mess of mistruths that claim I am not valuable enough to matter. My mind knows I matter to you, but what a battle to process truth when feelings of abandonment and unworthiness suffocate my heart.

Lord, please touch the lonely so we know you're still there. I know you are, but right now I'd like to hear from the one who gave his life for me. Thank you that I matter to you. Thank you for always sticking by me.

I look for someone to come and help me, but no one gives me a passing thought! No one will help me; no one cares a bit what happens to me. Then I pray to you, O LORD. I say, "You are my place of refuge. You are all I really want in life."

PSALM 142:4-5

☀ **A prayer about DEFEAT**
When my child needs to win

LORD,

Our sweet child needs to be victorious at something. I know you hurt to see his pain, just as I do. Winning isn't everything, and he definitely is learning tenacity through this. But sometimes we all just need a big WIN. He needs one. He needs to see that his efforts do pay off, that he can work hard and gain something of value.

Lord, show him the success he can be when he trusts you fully. Please grow a solid, victorious faith in him that wins for you even if the world doesn't call him a winner. Brace him for life's struggles, for the defeat that will come at times. But Lord, let his victories as your child mean so much more to him. May your complete acceptance of him heal and motivate his heart for your pursuits. I believe in you both, and I'm asking you to take him far in you. Thank you so much for loving him even more than I do.

Every child of God defeats this evil world, and we achieve this victory through our faith. And who can win this battle against the world? Only those who believe that Jesus is the Son of God. 1 JOHN 5:4-5

☀ A prayer about RENEWAL
When I need the hope of a new beginning

GOD,

Everywhere I ventured today, I seemed to be surrounded by my reflection in mirrors, windowpanes, and glass-covered pictures. I confess that much of what I saw I did not like. The images were painful reminders that nothing stays the same. Everything in this world is constantly deteriorating and wasting away, including me. Youthful energy and exterior beauty are fleeting.

God, daily I am tempted to give up and let everything go because chasing after the dream of consistency is a waste of time. I need the hope you give for renewal. I want your supernatural makeover of my life, marriage, family, and world. I certainly cannot see your plan for restoration, but I trust that you are always at work accomplishing your will. I remember, Lord, that things are not the way you created them to be because of the Fall. And I know that thanks to you, they are not like they will be. One day you will make all things new.

We never give up. Though our bodies are dying, our spirits are being renewed every day. 2 CORINTHIANS 4:16

⚙ **A prayer about REGRETS**
When I am prone to doubts

FATHER,

Should I have given this to my child? Would she be better off if we had taken a different direction? Could I have been a better mother to my daughter the other day when she came to me with her questions? Doubts and regrets plague me over things that might have happened, that could have happened. Please, Father, give me your strength to bring all these fears and misgivings to you. You alone have the power to change my thinking and give me wisdom to take these thoughts captive to the obedience of Christ.

I want to relinquish all the thoughts that I am powerless to affect. Replace these reservations with the truth of your Word. Father, please comfort and reassure me, reminding me that you sovereignly love and care for my children more than I ever could. Renew my hope that you will complete the work you have started in my children and that whatever those works are, they are for their ultimate good. I need to remember that motherhood is about surrendering my plans and agendas and trusting in a better plan that you have ordained.

When doubts filled my mind, your comfort gave me renewed hope and cheer. PSALM 94:19

⚙ **A prayer about HOPE**
When I can't see beyond my circumstances

LORD JESUS,

I've been weighed down by doubt and disillusionment lately. What I had planned and expected has not worked out. But your Word assures me that you understand my discouragement and long to replace that with hope. Your plans for me *are* good, though I cannot yet see how. Today I ask for your comfort, your healing, your counsel, and your kindness. But most of all, I ask for the grace to look past my circumstances and into your heart toward me.

LORD, you know the hopes of the helpless. Surely you will hear their cries and comfort them. PSALM 10:17

⚙ **A prayer about CELEBRATION**
When I want to encourage daily rejoicing

JESUS,

How wonderful it is that those who know you as Savior have a daily reason to celebrate. In fact, you provide unending reasons to live with a joy-filled heart. Please help me model this grateful attitude to my children so that they will keep an eternal perspective even when day-to-day living is difficult.

You will show me the way of life, granting me the joy of your presence and the pleasures of living with you forever.
PSALM 16:11

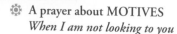

☼ A prayer about MOTIVES
When I am not looking to you

LORD JESUS,

"Because I said so." I remember vowing never to say these words to my own children, but I find myself doing it anyway. It's an easy default when I am tired and just want my children to obey. Sometimes I have good reasons for insisting that they follow my directions, but other times I am simply busy with something else or just want some quiet, and it is the easiest thing to say. I don't want to exert control over my children just because I am the mother. I want to take the opportunities to teach them how to make their own choices. The easy way out sometimes comes at a cost.

Help me to examine my motives when it comes to wanting my children to do what I say. Show me when I need to step back and allow them to make a mistake or a choice I wouldn't want them to make. Teach me how to guide them toward good choices.

The purpose of my instruction is that all believers would be filled with love that comes from a pure heart, a clear conscience, and genuine faith. 1 TIMOTHY 1:5

⛭ **A prayer about POTENTIAL**
When I have a hard time seeing what is possible

SPIRIT,

I stand today up to my knees in plenty of things that have potential—clothes that need to be folded, dishes that need to be washed, and projects that always seem to remain unfinished. I recognize lots of potential here, but there's not much hope of seeing any of them completed anytime soon.

Spirit, change my perspective to match yours. Help me to remember that you always see the finish line as you guide me through each day. You will complete your work in this world, and you will complete your work in me. I know part of that work is changing my attitudes and actions about all that lies undone in my life. Forgive the many days I waste my time being discouraged and angry about not being in control of the timing and productivity of my life. I want to live as a mother who has a long-term, eternal viewpoint.

I am certain that God, who began the good work within you, will continue his work until it is finally finished on the day when Christ Jesus returns. PHILIPPIANS 1:6

☼ **A prayer about SAFETY**
   When I need a shelter to hide in

LORD,

In any given week, I feel as though I walk a hundred paths and drive a thousand miles. As I take a step in a new direction, I seldom even consider whether I will be safe or not. As I sit in traffic, I take for granted all the bad things that *didn't* happen while I was driving around town. You, O Lord, have ordained all my paths. You go before me and follow closely behind, hemming me in. You decide not only where I go but also all the human interactions I will have. Are those with whom I surround myself pursuing righteous or wicked things? Often I am unsure of their motivations.

   Lord, help me depend on you daily for guidance and discernment. Give me wisdom to follow your sovereign path for my day. Give me sensitivity to listen and judge rightly as I relate to others. Lord, all of my safety and security rest squarely in your hands. I am thankful and at peace that I can rest in this safe refuge.

The name of the LORD is a strong fortress; the godly run to him and are safe. PROVERBS 18:10

DAY 214

☀ **A prayer about BROKENNESS**
   When I need restoration

LORD,

The world tells me to be self-sufficient, to be independent, to never let 'em see me sweat. But that's a whole lot of pressure that you don't ask me to handle. Yes, you ask me to be brave—in your power. You ask me to trust. And you bless the broken. But I have trouble being convinced of those truths because I've been indoctrinated with the language of a world that prides itself . . . well, on itself.

One of your methods for helping me unlearn these faulty perspectives on life is by letting me get worn down to the point of brokenness. That's where you can really work true maturity in me. That's where you grow your strength in me. That's where I see you more clearly. Thank you for not leaving me in the place of brokenness. Please radiate through my weakness so my children learn to value the preciousness of a season of brokenness in your care.

The high and lofty one who lives in eternity, the Holy One, says this: "I live in the high and holy place with those whose spirits are contrite and humble. I restore the crushed spirit of the humble and revive the courage of those with repentant hearts." ISAIAH 57:15

☼ A prayer about ADAPTABILITY
When I need patience to restructure my day

GOD,

Aagghh! Can I get that off my chest first thing? Secondly, I'd like to thank you for not freaking out when I do. I'm bringing my most high-maintenance emotions to you now, but I'm so grateful that you're God and you can handle . . . *me.*

Lord, my patience feels stretched thin because my plans have been rearranged yet again. I'm not sure how I'll finish the original things on my schedule because unexpected needs keep popping up. You know that old saying "A mother's work is never done"? Well, that's because she keeps inheriting more tasks from everyone else. She's expected to be ready and willing to adapt at a second's notice. I love my family, but at the moment these extra interruptions have me frazzled. So again, God, I thank you for always handling my changing needs. While you never change, you're always able to hold me as I bounce around in constant adaptation. Thank you for not treating me like an interruption. Please grant me extra grace and adaptability to pass on to my loved ones so they sense your style of welcome from me.

Even though I am a free man with no master, I have become a slave to all people to bring many to Christ.
I CORINTHIANS 9:19

☀ A prayer about GRACE
When I need perspective

HEAVENLY FATHER,

My child gives me a fresh perspective on grace. No matter how many times he disobeys or doesn't listen, I still am overwhelmed with love for him. This must be how you feel about me. Thank you for being my loving Father.

Let us come boldly to the throne of our gracious God. There we will receive his mercy, and we will find grace to help us when we need it most. HEBREWS 4:16

DAY 217 *Prayerful Moment*

☀ A prayer about WORK
When I forget where laziness will lead

HEAVENLY FATHER,

I long to instill in my children a strong work ethic. Not just because it is valued by the world but because it is a biblical principle. However, I know that our human nature drives all of us to seek the payoff without the labor. Please help my children to see that when they work hard for your glory, not only will they prosper, but more importantly, they will grow deeper in their relationship with you.

Lazy people want much but get little, but those who work hard will prosper. PROVERBS 13:4

☼ **A prayer about HEALTH**
When I need permission to put myself first

LORD,

I find myself spending so much time and energy worrying and caring for the well-being of my family that I often neglect my own body. You have given me this body to be cared for and treated as your temple, but I don't always take the time to care for it the way I should.

Remind me that it is not selfish to take time out for myself. Help me to slow down and make the effort to care for my body by giving it healthy food and activity to keep it strong and well. It is only through caring for myself that I can give my best self to my family. Thank you for this body and for the strength you give me each day.

Don't you realize that your body is the temple of the Holy Spirit, who lives in you and was given to you by God? You do not belong to yourself, for God bought you with a high price. So you must honor God with your body.

1 CORINTHIANS 6:19-20

☼ A prayer about TEMPTATION
When I am enticed

PRECIOUS SAVIOR,

Why does losing weight seem so difficult? I have faced this battle alone for too many years. Thank you, Jesus, for bringing into my life other mothers who are pursuing the same goals. Please help us to encourage one another daily. May we partner together to exercise self-control in our eating. I know we all desire to glorify you with our bodies, but the temptations surrounding bad habits seem to lurk at every turn. Please show us creative ways to address our bad behaviors and replace them with healthy ones.

When we are faced with enticements, fill us with your Spirit so we can overcome them by faith. Give us small encouragements of progress so that we will persevere together. I know that ultimately the need to lose weight and pursue a healthier lifestyle indicates a deeply rooted spiritual problem. Help us to discover the root issues that cause us to yield to temptations. Today may we all practice physical and spiritual disciplines with a renewed commitment to follow closely after you.

Dear brothers and sisters, if another believer is overcome by some sin, you who are godly should gently and humbly help that person back onto the right path. And be careful not to fall into the same temptation yourself.

GALATIANS 6:1

☀ **A prayer about BEAUTY**
When I want to glow with spiritual loveliness

LORD,

Beauty that comes from within is rare, but it never ceases to leave an impression. Regardless of whether someone is outwardly stunning or plain, Christlikeness filtering from the inside out can transform someone's physical appearance. It's downright irresistible. I want that kind of beauty, and I want my children to prize it too. May they grow up in a home where they fall in love with the beauty of who you are.

I think about the Old Testament sisters Leah and Rachel, who shared the unfortunate situation of having the same husband, one who didn't love them equally. Lord, that would have been a very bitter pill to swallow. Their circumstances did not bring out the best in either of them, and I wonder how they might have improved their lives if they'd loved you wholeheartedly. Over time, Rachel's bitterness surely marred her physical beauty, and real loveliness may have made over Leah's plainness if she'd only basked in your goodness with her whole self. Who knows? True beauty could even have won over her husband's heart. I want true beauty with no regrets, Lord.

You should clothe yourselves instead with the beauty that comes from within, the unfading beauty of a gentle and quiet spirit, which is so precious to God. I PETER 3:4

☼ A prayer about REFRESHMENT
When I need a break

LORD,

You know that I often feel as though I can't get enough of my children. They amaze me every day with their growing bodies, their curious minds, their tender hearts. But since I know you want me to be honest with you, God, here it is: Sometimes I do feel as if I've had enough of these precious, frustrating creatures. Sometimes I would like a break from them. Not permanently, but for a time—an hour, a day, or even a weekend. It's good to miss them every now and then.

I imagine whiling away a whole thirty minutes, being quiet with you or rediscovering the organized thoughts I still believe are gasping for air somewhere in my overloaded mother-brain.

Thank you, Lord, for understanding my limits and needs, just as I try to understand and meet my children's needs. Today please help my heart to rest in yours. Please quiet my spirit even if the day does not allow for a pause. Thank you for not being shocked by the truth. And thanks again, Father, for these sweet kids.

The LORD replied, "I will personally go with you, . . . and I will give you rest." EXODUS 33:14

☼ A prayer about HELPLESSNESS
When there is nothing I can do

FATHER,

I feel so powerless. I am faced with an impossible situation and do not know where to turn to find a solution. Why is it that it's only when I get to the end of myself that I think to turn to you? I so easily forget that you are the only one who can see a way out of this. Only you have the power to make a way where there doesn't seem to be one.

Forgive me for not turning to you sooner. Please help me in this situation. Help me to give my control over to you and to trust you to bring it all together for good. Help me to be patient and wait on your timing. You are my Father, and you want nothing but the best for me. Even though I can't see why this is happening, you know why and you know best. Help me to lean into you and have faith in you.

The Holy Spirit helps us in our weakness. For example, we don't know what God wants us to pray for. But the Holy Spirit prays for us with groanings that cannot be expressed in words. And the Father who knows all hearts knows what the Spirit is saying, for the Spirit pleads for us believers in harmony with God's own will. ROMANS 8:26-27

☼ A prayer about BOUNDARIES
When my kids want more freedom

FATHER,

Please help me teach my kids what true freedom involves. Help them understand that the boundaries I set, based on the Bible's standards, are actually designed to help them live *freely* instead of falling into the prison of sin. Impress this truth on their hearts in a way that makes it their own.

You have been called to live in freedom, my brothers and sisters. But don't use your freedom to satisfy your sinful nature. Instead, use your freedom to serve one another in love.
GALATIANS 5:13

DAY 224 *Prayerful Moment*

☼ A prayer about INTIMACY
When I want to learn to be open

LORD,

You have created me to be in community—to connect with others at a deep heart level. This is a value I want to instill in my children. I don't want them to fear intimacy but to embrace others. Help me to model this by tearing down any walls I may have subconsciously erected to keep others at arm's length. May my children learn how to develop and maintain healthy friendships and relationships by watching me.

Love each other with genuine affection, and take delight in honoring each other. ROMANS 12:10

DAY 225

☼ **A prayer about ADVERSITY**
  When I see my kids struggle

LORD,

I don't suppose my own pain hurts me quite the same as my children's troubles do. When I watch my kids struggle, I often feel inadequate to know what to say, how to help, or whether to simply be quietly available. As my children mature, I wonder how I will know my role in each phase of their lives. As a child grows up, so does a parent. Lord, I'm feeling growing pains right along with them. If there were a fix-it switch, life would be so much easier. One flip of it, and all would be well.

But then we wouldn't have the chance to grow our faith in you, would we? Hmm. Maybe faith growth is part of what you're helping us learn through adversity. Please show my children through this struggle that you are always with them and ready to help. Draw them close to know you more fully; deepening intimacy with you will make this challenge mean something. Help them rely on you to fight with them and for them. Mature their faith and character so that you shine through them in a world of adversity.

God is our refuge and strength, always ready to help in times of trouble. PSALM 46:1

❋ A prayer about TENDERNESS
When I crave the compassionate love of a father

FATHER,

Thank you for the tender way you love me. At times I have difficulty extending that same compassion to my children. I remember with pain the lack of tenderness and love I received from my earthly father. Now, many years later, I still bear the wounds and scars from that undelivered affection.

Give me grace, *heavenly* Father, to break the cycle of graceless relationships. You alone are the reference point for healthy relationships. I know I will grow in my appreciation and application of this type of gentle care only as I study the Scriptures. From cover to cover you have dealt patiently with your sinful children. And I see myself in those pages, especially when I have been stiff-necked and cold in my response to you. You have extended kindheartedness and grace my way. Forgive me for the many ways I have refused or withheld my love from others. May the model of your unfailing love be the legacy of my family, not only for this generation but also for future generations.

The LORD is like a father to his children, tender and compassionate to those who fear him. PSALM 103:13

☼ **A prayer about GOD'S WORD**
When I fill my mind with good things

LORD,

You have entrusted me not only with a young life to care for but also with my own life. You have put me in this position so that I can live a life worthy of you and share your love with others. One way for me to live a healthy life is to read your Word and try to align my life with your purposes. By filling my mind and heart with your truth, I can honor you with my life.

Help me remember to spend time in your Word daily and to share your words with my children as they grow. Let your truth shine through my life as I reflect your character. Help me to instill your truth and love in everyone I encounter.

My child, pay attention to what I say. Listen carefully to my words. Don't lose sight of them. Let them penetrate deep into your heart, for they bring life to those who find them, and healing to their whole body. Guard your heart above all else, for it determines the course of your life.

PROVERBS 4:20-23

☀ A prayer about EMPTINESS
When I need to know you're enough

LORD,

I think I could dwell on today's verses forever. I want more of you, more power to understand the vastness of your love. I want more completeness and fullness that comes from soaking up your Spirit.

I'm not sure how it happens, how you fill a mere human with yourself. But I'm so grateful that you were aware of my emptiness before I was. Lord, whatever it takes, fill me. I don't want to waste my days when you are ready and willing to instill me with your abundance. Glorify yourself in my lack by showing yourself strong and merciful. Show me how wide, long, high, and deep your love for my family and me is. Make yourself real to each of us in new ways this week. Make your home in us as we long for the eternal home you're making to share with us.

Christ will make his home in your hearts as you trust in him. Your roots will grow down into God's love and keep you strong. And may you have the power to understand, as all God's people should, how wide, how long, how high, and how deep his love is. May you experience the love of Christ, though it is too great to understand fully. Then you will be made complete with all the fullness of life and power that comes from God. EPHESIANS 3:17-19

☼ **A prayer about COMPARISON**
When I forget that I don't have to be perfect

HEAVENLY FATHER,

I waste so much energy trying to be what I think a good mother should be. I compare myself to other mothers and their seemingly perfect children and feel like a failure. I am simply unable to measure up to the bar that the media, the church, and the world seem to set.

But you don't want me to be like anyone else. You created me to be unique. Your Word says that I am fearfully and wonderfully made. You made me—each and every facet of me—from the very beginning. You designed each part of me for a specific purpose. Yet it is hard for me to embrace the things about myself that seem less than ideal. Help me to trust in you and see myself through your eyes. Remind me every day that you love me just the way I am.

You made all the delicate, inner parts of my body and knit me together in my mother's womb. Thank you for making me so wonderfully complex! Your workmanship is marvelous—how well I know it. PSALM 139:13-14

☼ **A prayer about QUIETNESS**
  When silence is golden

GOD,

I have lived in my van, chasing my children's schedules across many city blocks. I sit at red lights, wondering what I have really accomplished. Even though my life tells the story that activity is what I crave, all I really want is silence. God, please carve out moments of silence for me so that I might soak in your presence and then reflect your goodness.

Better to have one handful with quietness than two handfuls with hard work and chasing the wind.
ECCLESIASTES 4:6

☼ **A prayer about PANIC**
  When I need a reminder that God cares

LORD,

I feel so alone. I wonder if anyone even sees my tears or hears my cries. But you tell me in your Word that you capture every one of my tears in a bottle. You see my pain and promise to walk with me through it. Calm my body and quiet my racing thoughts. I have nowhere else to turn. Thank you that you will never abandon or forsake me.

You keep track of all my sorrows. You have collected all my tears in your bottle. You have recorded each one in your book.
PSALM 56:8

☀ A prayer about ETERNITY
When I long for its freedom

GOD,

I long to praise you forever, starting now! These days, Lord, I'm wishing hard for forever to begin immediately. How I'd love for my children to be spared the troubles of this life. Yes, life here can be wonderful, but it can also be loaded with troubles. How much better for your children to be with you. Sometimes I have such a tough time waiting for Jesus' return. Even when I get caught up with the details of life on earth, there's still a part of my heart that longs for what's missing. This discontent isn't going to be relieved for good until I can enjoy heaven with you.

I want my kids to long for eternity as well. Please give them forever-focus instead of living caught up in the here and now that is fading away. Plant in us hearts of praise and thanks, and help us worship you with our lives. Thank you for offering forever and for making a way through Jesus for us to share eternity with you. We have no idea just how good it will be, do we? Thank you for the glimpses of heaven that you give us in your Word. They are the source of true hope while we wait for someday.

O LORD my God, I will give you thanks forever!
PSALM 30:12

☼ A prayer about SATISFACTION
When I desire a thankful heart

FATHER,

My teenage boy seems to always be hungry—there's no limit to his appetite. Some days, I wonder if he will eat us out of house and home. As a young man, he also hungers for entertainment, relationships, and success. These pursuits exhaust him. Contentment can be difficult to come by. But he is not alone in his vain pursuits; I am following these things right alongside him. I often find myself restless and unsatisfied with my life.

Father, forgive me for my unhappiness and lead me in the way of thanksgiving and gratefulness. Help me to perceive the blessings in each day. Give us occasions to spur one another on to see your daily provisions. Please cultivate in our family a culture of gratitude. May our mouths and hearts overflow with praise for your many sweet provisions.

Everything is wearisome beyond description. No matter how much we see, we are never satisfied. No matter how much we hear, we are not content. ECCLESIASTES 1:8

☼ A prayer about ADVICE
When I catch myself talking too much

LORD,

I caught myself talking to a friend like a self-proclaimed pro. I spoke on and on as if my thoughts were a gold mine of blessing to anyone I could catch listening. You heard me too, God. My mouth just kept rattling on about the benefits of *this*, the warning signs of *that*, the rumors about *them*, and what my friend should do about *it*. You'd think I knew all that and more. Well, you wouldn't be fooled, because you know better about me, God. Most likely, my friend knows the truth about me too. My penchant for giving advice is not attractive when I let it run amok. But it's so easy to offer too much too often and attempt to pass it off as "sharing information."

Please remind me that too much talk inevitably will reveal my foolishness. Help me to listen abundantly yet speak sparingly. Please keep me so occupied listening for your Spirit that my mouth doesn't have time to verbalize every tidbit I think someone else could benefit from. And Lord, if someone wants my advice, please speak through me so it's you they hear.

A fool's proud talk becomes a rod that beats him.
PROVERBS 14:3

☼ A prayer about DECISIONS
When I need clear direction

GOD,

If only there was a manual for this. You see the options in front of me, as well as my confusion about which path to take. I wish I could know your perfect direction every time so I could relax about this decision. I've been weighing it all so much that I'm not sure of anything anymore except the size of my doubts. I don't want to jump ahead of you or lag behind, and I definitely don't want to wind up on a path that you aren't leading me on.

I'm ready to act, Lord, but if I don't sense your clear answer, please help me to stay the course until I can tell you're moving me one way or another. And God? Please don't let me miss your voice. Give me better ears to hear you. I'm claiming your promise that you will draw near to me when I draw near to you. I especially need you on this one, Lord, so thank you in advance for helping me understand your guidance.

Your own ears will hear him. Right behind you a voice will say, "This is the way you should go," whether to the right or to the left. ISAIAH 30:21

❁ A prayer about HOSPITALITY
When I want to show your love

LORD,

As my children grow, I want my home to be a welcoming environment for their friends. Some of these kids may not have experienced your love and grace in their own families. Our home may be the only exposure they have to a safe and nurturing place. Help me to create a space in our home that is inviting. Remind me, even when I am tired, that laughter and messes are a part of life and the value of being hospitable trumps having a clean house. Help me to show each child who graces my doorstep the same love and attention I give my own. Remind me that even those I find hard to love are loved dearly by you.

Show me how to teach my kids this same value of hospitality. Guide them to make wise choices as they make friends so that they are surrounding themselves with positive influences and are able to positively influence others.

Share your food with the hungry, and give shelter to the homeless. Give clothes to those who need them, and do not hide from relatives who need your help. ISAIAH 58:7

☼ **A prayer about GOD'S WISDOM**
When I need godly insight

SPIRIT OF GOD,
I confess that sometimes I am more concerned that my children be smart than that they be wise. Knowledge acquired is great, but knowledge applied is even better. May all of us seek to revere you and to stand in awe of your ways. As we grow in our appreciation for your character, may that be evident in our decisions and choices. Holy Spirit, please keep us in steadfast pursuit of godly insights.

Fear of the LORD is the foundation of true knowledge, but fools despise wisdom and discipline. PROVERBS 1:7

DAY 238 *Prayerful Moment*

☼ **A prayer about TIME**
When I long to make the most of every moment

LORD,
I lose count of how many people I encounter as I walk from the train to my office. I long to walk in wisdom, managing my time, words, and actions in a way that pleases you. I want my life to have an eternal impact in the souls of others. I lay down my plans and agenda and look to you to ordain my steps.

Live wisely among those who are not believers, and make the most of every opportunity. COLOSSIANS 4:5

☼ **A prayer about CRITICISM**
When I need a good reply for a belittler

LORD,

Sometimes I wish it would be okay with you if I replied to someone's derogatory words with similar words of my own! I know, I do spout off in retaliation now and then, but each time, I realize later that my choice did not honor you or help the situation. Part of my desire to set someone straight comes from an unholy voice that says I have a right to defend myself and put others in their place. And oh, it feels good for a moment. But then it doesn't. When I remember that you're most pleased when I delight in you, I don't care so much about what others say.

Please help me live beyond someone else's smallness that shows up as belittling criticism. Please give me a vision of that soul as seen through your eyes; it is a soul so precious to you that you died to give him or her life, just as you did for me. Help me to respond more generously than by belittling, but not with arrogance. Help me offer grace in response to rudeness, mercy in place of criticism, as I stand strong and whole in you.

"Don't sin by letting anger control you." Don't let the sun go down while you are still angry, for anger gives a foothold to the devil. EPHESIANS 4:26-27

☼ A prayer about GUILT
When I need to find a new way to motivate

GRACIOUS FATHER,

As a mother, I find myself using guilt as a way to manipulate my children into doing what I want. I see myself doing it and know it is wrong, but I do it anyway. Sometimes it just seems to be the easiest way to deal with an issue. This is not a pattern I want to pass along to my children. I want them to treat others with kindness and respect, and not manipulate to get their way. Help me to model the kind of behavior you have modeled for me. Help me to stop myself midsentence when I find myself leaning toward using guilt as a tool. Remind me once again to embrace kindness, goodness, gentleness, and self-control in my dealings with everyone, but especially in my role as a mother as I mold and shape my children. Thank you for being the role model I can follow in my parenting every day.

Repent of your sins and turn to God, so that your sins may be wiped away. Then times of refreshment will come from the presence of the Lord, and he will again send you Jesus, your appointed Messiah. ACTS 3:19-20

⚙ **A prayer about REST**
When I resist the invitation of Christ

FATHER,

I come to the end of my day weary, discouraged, and physically exhausted. Yet my soul is quiet now, and I can hear your gentle, gracious, and personal invitation to come. Why do I resist this sweet call? Forgive me, Lord, for being distracted by the concerns of this world and captivated by the good things rather than what is best. Your invitation is so full of promise that I can begin to feel hope swelling within me. I am grateful your invitation is constant and continual. It is not conditional; it is for every weary soul.

Father, show me what resting and abiding in you means. I need to come, lay my burdens down, and open my hands and heart to you. I want to receive, to have my deepest hunger and thirst satisfied, and to accept your will for my life. Father, with all you are calling me to do tomorrow, may I rest while I run? Thank you, precious Lord, for your promise of true rest and Sabbath. Restore my heart, renew my mind, and reinvigorate my strength to follow you another day.

Jesus said, "Come to me, all of you who are weary and carry heavy burdens, and I will give you rest."
MATTHEW 11:28

☼ A prayer about LONELINESS
When I want to fix it

HEAVENLY FATHER,

It is so hard for me to watch my child struggle with loneliness. Seeing her hurt when her friends are mean to her or don't invite her to activities makes me want to jump in and protect her. I know that I can't always be there to make things better. I can't force others to include her and treat her kindly in all situations. Life is hard, and learning how to deal with rejection is a fact of life I can't shield her from.

Even though I can't keep her from experiencing pain, you have promised that you will always walk with her. You will comfort and provide a refuge for her when life gets hard. Thank you for always being there too. Help me to teach my child to lean on you and trust you during the painful times when it feels like no one cares. Enable her to stand on the truth that you will never leave her.

Even when I walk through the darkest valley, I will not be afraid, for you are close beside me. Your rod and your staff protect and comfort me. PSALM 23:4

☀ **A prayer about APOLOGY**
When I need to "fess up"

GOD,

I had to ask my children's forgiveness. I let my emotions rule, my temper flare, my mouth spout, and my heart reveal its uglier side. At first I didn't realize that I needed to apologize to them; I'm the mother, after all, and they need to learn not to push my buttons, right?

But then I felt your nudge in my spirit, and I knew that excuse wouldn't measure up to your desire that I live honestly and reflect your character. When I said I was sorry for how I had spoken to them, they didn't deny what I'd done. They knew as well as I did that I had messed up. Lord, thank you for not letting me get away with modeling deception and unkindness to them. Even though they saw me choose unwisely at first, please let them learn from my mistake and know that they need to offer honest apologies when they mess up as well. Thank you, Lord, for a lesson learned—and for your merciful method of getting me back on track.

People who conceal their sins will not prosper, but if they confess and turn from them, they will receive mercy.
PROVERBS 28:13

☀ **A prayer about LIFE'S DEMANDS**
   When I need a break

LORD,

Today I am so tired of the pressure from commitments at school and church, as well as deadlines at work. I can't do it all by myself. I need your help, strength, and direction. Thank you for the invitation to cast all my cares on you. Now give me the grace to accept it!

Give all your worries and cares to God, for he cares about you.
I PETER 5:7

DAY 245 *Prayerful Moment*

☀ **A prayer about BOREDOM**
   When I struggle with my children's attitudes

LORD,

I'm so tired of hearing "I'm bored"! It's never said gently; it's always with a whine. Please, Lord, grow my children's gratitude and enliven them with your presence to counteract the doldrums of feeling they have nothing to do. Help me encourage them to serve rather than waiting to be served, as you modeled. Life is exciting when it's lived through and for you.

Since the world began, no ear has heard and no eye has seen a God like you, who works for those who wait for him!
ISAIAH 64:4

☼ **A prayer about OBEDIENCE**
When I need a fresh perspective

LORD JESUS,

So many times I feel irritation building inside me because my child just will not listen to me. All I am asking is that he respect my authority so that he can avoid hurt in the long run. Why is it so hard for him to listen?

Wait a minute. I have to sit back and smile. How often have I childishly rebelled against your authority and blocked out your voice so that I could have my own way? And how many times have I found myself in pain because I refused to listen? Remind me of my own disobedience and help me to give my child grace, just as you have given grace to me. You have forgiven me more times than I can count, and you continue to patiently guide me—whether I listen to you or not. Help me to learn from your holy example and grow in my own patience today.

Peter came to him and asked, "Lord, how often should I forgive someone who sins against me? Seven times?" "No, not seven times," Jesus replied, "but seventy times seven!"
MATTHEW 18:21-22

☼ A prayer about FEAR
When doubt shouts louder than faith

LORD,

I want to hear your calm assurances, but fear shouts so loudly sometimes and feeds my doubt instead of my faith. Some of my greatest fears involve my kids because I can't keep them from all harm. Freak accidents, predators, illnesses, unexpected disasters—all are out of my control, and it scares me to think of my precious children's wholeness being endangered.

But Jesus, for generations you've helped parents who've faced horrendously fearful situations with their young ones. Jairus felt the roller coaster of emotions when his little daughter neared death. He allowed his hope to grow when he approached you. When you seemed too late, Jairus's heart may have crashed. But you were there all along, and you were not late or unhelpful. You tell me to entrust my children to you. Thank you, Lord, that even though the din of fear is loud, you are exceedingly more powerful—and fully confident of your ability to guard their lives. So I place my children once again in your hands, where they've been most safe all along. Please grant me grace to trust you more than my fears.

Jesus overheard them and said to Jairus, "Don't be afraid. Just have faith." MARK 5:36

✿ **A prayer about CHANGE**
When I feel unsure of what's coming

LORD,

Change is one of those phenomena that can feel like a huge blessing or a dreaded prison. Sometimes change can bring refreshment from a draining season; other times it can shake us out of a very cozy lifestyle into one that doesn't feel like such a good fit. And then there's the kind of change you do inside of us, which typically brings a sting or two as we awaken to a flawed character trait. When you change us, you often require that we do something differently in response—your change in us begets change from us.

But God, when you initiate a change, we can take comfort that the new thing you're doing is for our good. In the end we'll be better for it. That truth brings huge peace despite the loss of familiarity, the nudge from my comfort zone, or the ache of addressing personal sin. So God, keep changing me. But while you're at it, would you please work a teachable, open spirit in me so that I welcome the goodness you're creating?

We know that God causes everything to work together for the good of those who love God and are called according to his purpose for them. ROMANS 8:28

✳ A prayer about TOUCH
When I am tempted to miss God's healing presence

FATHER,

I go about my errands today a weak and wounded woman. The demands of my family and the pressures of deadlines cause me great anguish. I need your fresh and holy touch. I know as I commune with you in prayer that healing is near. I know that through the peace-filled truths I find in your Word, my soul may rest. I am thankful to sense your presence in the midst of community. My brothers and sisters in Christ are tangible reminders of your power to heal. They are your hands, feet, and voice in my place of trouble.

Father, I ask your forgiveness for the countless ways I try to anesthetize my pain. I try to hide or run to lesser things. I can never escape from your presence, and I cannot conceal your ever-present gaze. Healing and wholeness are only possible through a meaningful encounter with you. Please renew my hope and draw me nearer to you today.

Jesus came over and touched them. "Get up," he said. "Don't be afraid." MATTHEW 17:7

⚙ **A prayer about WORK**
When I need to cease from my labors

GOD,

Looking over my calendar, I am absolutely overwhelmed with the senseless number of activities that I am involved in through the year. I have allowed our family to become overcommitted yet again. We have no margin in our schedules to rest and to be renewed. I acknowledge that this is more than poor planning; it is sin. I repent of not valuing the pattern of Sabbath rest. You have set the pattern for us all on how life optimally functions. My desire to please others and accomplish worldly success has clouded my judgment and choices.

Please help me remember, Lord, that every choice to do something good is also a choice to not do something that may be better. I want to model for my children a healthy rhythm of life that pleases you. Please strengthen me to address undesirable patterns in my schedule. God, I commit to you this week that I will rest from my labors and then rest unto you this Lord's day. Give me grace to lay aside entanglements that sideline me from serving you with my whole heart.

On the seventh day God had finished his work of creation, so he rested from all his work. GENESIS 2:2

☀ A prayer about CONFLICT
When sibling rivalry rules our home

JESUS,

They're at it again. Instead of being each other's first friend, a safety net of mutual support, my kids are bickering and tearing each other down. It hurts me to watch it, and it threatens to darken the atmosphere of our home. Please soften their hearts toward each other and open their eyes to each other's wonderful characteristics. Help them grow in patience and graciousness so that we as a family may bless one another.

Confess your sins to each other and pray for each other so that you may be healed. JAMES 5:16

☀ A prayer about UNITY
When I want to overlook my own sin

LORD,

Why can't my friend understand how she has hurt my feelings? To me this offense is as clear as day. I know at times I can be blind to the potential for peacemaking because of the enormity of my sin. Help me to consider the speck in my sister's eye as nothing. Give me grace to move toward her, pursuing understanding.

Hypocrite! First get rid of the log in your own eye; then you will see well enough to deal with the speck in your friend's eye.
MATTHEW 7:5

☼ **A prayer about OBSTACLES**
When I find myself off course

LORD,

I don't like it when my plans are thwarted. Whether it is the unexpected flat tire, a sudden illness, or an unplanned expense, there are days when I feel like all I am doing is running into walls. It is easy to feel like you are against me and are the author of my problems. But that is far from the case.

You are my champion and Savior. You walk with me through all of my challenges, big and small. Help me to remember that I am not doing life alone. You are with me every step of the way. Remind me that I am making progress every day, despite any setbacks that I encounter. Mold me into the person you want me to be through the unexpected issues I face.

When your faith remains strong through many trials, it will bring you much praise and glory and honor on the day when Jesus Christ is revealed to the whole world. I PETER 1:7

☀ **A prayer about HONESTY**
When I want to be a good example

HEAVENLY FATHER,

One of the most important things I want to pass along to my child is the value of integrity. I know that the only way to do this is to model it in my own life. It is so easy to be tempted to stretch the truth or exaggerate a situation, but little eyes are watching every move I make and learning from my example.

Help me to root out any dishonesty that exists in my life. Help me to walk in your truth and model it to my little one. You have given me the perfect example of how to live out integrity in my interactions. Mold me and shape me into an accurate reflection of your character. Help me to pass along these values as my child grows and learns to love you.

Stop telling lies. Let us tell our neighbors the truth, for we are all parts of the same body. EPHESIANS 4:25

☼ A prayer about COMMUNICATION
When I struggle to discipline with respect

LORD,

We're speaking two different languages in our house. My kids and I aren't on the same page these days, and I'm beyond myself to know how to connect with them on their level while maintaining my authority. I want them to feel respected just as I want to be respected. How do I communicate in a way that validates their feelings and builds them up, even when I have to draw a tough line? How do I show them that I do hear and care about what they're saying but that my decision is final?

Please give me greater vision into their world. Help me to listen well, using both my ears and my heart. Please enable my children and me to understand one another's views, and help us to stick with each other so we can reap the benefits of learning to communicate better. I know the effort will pay off, even though our conversations sometimes leave me feeling drained now.

The words of the godly encourage many, but fools are destroyed by their lack of common sense.

PROVERBS 10:21

✴ A prayer about BOUNDARIES
When people-pleasing becomes a habit

LORD,

I caught myself scrambling again to fit into a mold I thought would please someone else. I caught myself, but not in time. I answered too agreeably even though I knew my response didn't reflect my true heart, and now I feel that familiar knot in the pit of my stomach. Truth is, I love to make people happy. But I can't let unhealthy people-pleasing become habitual. I didn't want to say yes; I wanted to hold my course even though it would earn someone's disapproval. How am I going to raise kids who think for themselves when I still keep flimsy boundaries and get caught in the people-pleasing trap?

If they haven't already, my children eventually will notice that strain of unsureness in me. That "secret's out" feeling gets my pride because I want to be fully secure, while acting with grace when someone isn't satisfied with my boundaries. Lord, steady me with your graciousness, and confirm the boundaries you want me to enforce in my life.

Let your conversation be gracious and attractive so that you will have the right response for everyone.
COLOSSIANS 4:6

☀ **A prayer about PRIDE**
When I need to practice a little humility

GOD,

I am often tempted to live vicariously through my children. I love them so much—they are incredible! Forgive me for making my children and their accomplishments something that I consider ultimate rather than treating them as good gifts from your hand. I am often tempted to compare them to other children. I confess that sometimes I judge other parents and their children, which leads to self-righteousness.

Lord, teach me humility no matter what it takes. I want to forsake the pride I take in my children and my parenting and consider others as more important than my family and me. God, I acknowledge that every accomplishment, every gift or ability you have given to me or my children, and every moment of my parenting is a gift from your hand and is possible only by your strength. Instead of envying other families, would you allow me the opportunity to serve them? Instead of judging other families, would you give me an opportunity to show them compassion and grace? God, I sincerely pray that evidence of humility will begin to be apparent in my life. Then, perhaps I will start to be a reflection of who you are.

Pride ends in humiliation, while humility brings honor.
PROVERBS 29:23

☼ A prayer about FRIENDSHIP
When I need to remember to be inclusive

PRECIOUS FATHER,

You have created me for community, and I am so grateful for the friends who fill my life with love and laughter. Help me to be a good friend. Open my eyes to those around me—perhaps a new coworker or the mother I just met at my child's school—who may be lonely and in need of a friend. Help me to show your love to others.

[Jesus said,] "You didn't choose me. I chose you. I appointed you to go and produce lasting fruit, so that the Father will give you whatever you ask for, using my name. This is my command: Love each other." JOHN 15:16-17

☼ A prayer about HAPPINESS
When I am unsatisfied

HEAVENLY FATHER,

Hearing the giggles of my children as they run and play reminds me what happiness is. Thank you for giving me a tangible reminder of your joy in my life. Help me to take the time to play and enjoy life today. May I live each moment with sweet abandon, remembering that my life is in your hands.

Let the heavens be glad, and the earth rejoice! Tell all the nations, "The Lord reigns!" Let the sea and everything in it shout his praise! Let the fields and their crops burst out with joy! 1 CHRONICLES 16:31-32

☼ A prayer about ENDURANCE
When my kids face temptation

FATHER,

My emotions are jumbled right now. I hurt for my children, who are facing some big temptations, and I feel anxious to offer the support they need. I'm worried they'll cave to the pressure and do things that will cause them remorse later on. I don't want them to carry the burdens of regret. I have some of those, and how often I've grieved the "if onlys" of wondering how you would have blessed the right choices I failed to make. I learned some lessons the hard way, and oh, how I want them to be spared painful consequences!

You show your love in so many ways, Lord, and at times like these I am amazed that your love strengthens us to endure beyond our sin natures. Please grant that special strength to these precious kids of mine. Sharpen their hearts and minds to heed your Spirit's warnings. Show them your promised way through the temptation, help them choose the wise way of obedience, and grace them with endurance to stick to your path.

The temptations in your life are no different from what others experience. And God is faithful. He will not allow the temptation to be more than you can stand. When you are tempted, he will show you a way out so that you can endure. I CORINTHIANS 10:13

☀ A prayer about AFFIRMATION
When I long to hear that I'm worthwhile

GOD,

You are Lord of the universe and the author of salvation. How is it possible that you notice me? Isaiah 43:1 says you speak personally to me by name, and I choose to believe you. I want to know that I'm yours. I'm here and I'm listening. Sometimes I think I'm improving at recognizing the holy hush of your Spirit whispering to mine. I love to hear from you, but I especially love your voice when you affirm to me that I belong to you. You tell me to listen up, and then you speak such comfort about my identity in you. You don't address me with "Hey you!" Instead, you call me by name, so intimately. You yourself attest to my worth, and my heart needs to hear your approval. If no one else offers it, I know you still do. Thank you for the affirmations in your Word that will continue to speak to future generations. Thank you for doing the hard work of ransoming me; I was lost apart from you. Please continue forming me as your own.

But now, O Jacob, listen to the LORD who created you. O Israel, the one who formed you says, "Do not be afraid, for I have ransomed you. I have called you by name; you are mine." ISAIAH 43:1

☼ A prayer about REWARDS
When I don't see my children as the gifts they are

FATHER,

All day long I have heard the cries of my children: "I want this!" "I need it!" "Help me with this!" "It's not fair!" I am struggling to see their exclamations as a blessing rather than a burden. You could give me many things, Father, that might seem good for a moment—such as a good meal out or a needed vacation—but none of these would ever measure up to the gift of my children. They have blessed me by their kindness and patience with me as their mother. They have shown me aspects of your character that I had long forgotten. They walk with me daily in this journey toward sanctification and knowing you. They have taught me the many facets of unconditional love and have demonstrated this virtue to me on countless occasions when I did not deserve it.

Father, forgive me for taking them for granted and for failing to appreciate so many of their unique qualities. Please enlarge my heart to treasure and prize my children as the true gifts from you that they are.

Children are a gift from the LORD; they are a reward from him. PSALM 127:3

☀ A prayer about MISTAKES
When I fall down again

LORD,

As much as I hate to admit it, failure is inevitable. We all find ourselves failing in one area or another, sometimes daily. I can so easily waste time beating myself up for falling short yet again.

But then I look at my children and the mistakes they are making. You gently nudge me and remind me that mistakes are necessary for growth. Forgetting to wear sunscreen and dealing with the resulting sunburn, deciding to wait until the night before to do a ten-page term paper, or wearing a tank top and shorts when it's twenty-eight degrees outside—each of these is a choice that may result in hard consequences but that can teach a lesson. Help me to not only allow my children the freedom to make mistakes, but also to extend grace to them when they fall. After all, that is what you do for me.

The godly may trip seven times, but they will get up again. But one disaster is enough to overthrow the wicked.

PROVERBS 24:16

☼ A prayer about QUITTING
When I want to resign from life

FATHER,

Where do I go to file my resignation letter? I am so frustrated that all of my jobs seem to be endless. For once I would love to actually complete a task from start to finish. Lord, I want to run and hide from everybody and everything that is crowding my life. But where can I go? No matter how far I try to run, I can never escape your glance. Thankfully, I am never far from your Spirit. And I can never escape from your presence. And though I feel trapped and cornered in this calling today, I know that your rescue and renewal for my heart are ever close.

Father, forgive me that all I could see today were burdens instead of blessings. My husband, my children, and my home are truly gifts from your hand. Lord, please grant me perseverance to stay engaged with the life you have called me to live.

I can never escape from your Spirit! I can never get away from your presence! PSALM 139:7

☼ **A prayer about EXCUSES**
When my heart and ears are filled with them

LORD,

You know when I'm making excuses, just as I know when my kids are doing it. Sometimes I still try to pass off my responsibility as if I were some kind of victim, even though the worm of deceit sickens me. Please help me live out wholehearted truth.

You will be proved right in what you say, and your judgment against me is just. . . . You desire honesty from the womb, teaching me wisdom even there. PSALM 51:4, 6

DAY 266 *Prayerful Moment*

☼ **A prayer about CHILDREN**
When I need to trust like they do

FATHER GOD,

Thank you for my kids, who remind me each day about simple faith that lets go and rests. My kids are so good at taking you at your Word. You said it; they believe it, and it provides security for their hearts. Help me to trust like they do, no matter what uncertainties this day holds.

I tell you the truth, unless you turn from your sins and become like little children, you will never get into the Kingdom of Heaven. MATTHEW 18:3

☀ A prayer about WEARINESS
When I am tempted to resign

HEAVENLY FATHER,

I fall into bed weary and exhausted. Today was a marathon parenting adventure filled with many unforeseen challenges. I feel as though I have spent my very last resource of emotional, physical, and spiritual energy. I desperately need you to refill me with your strength. As I lie still tonight, I remember that herein lies the key to replenishment—to be still, cease striving, and remember that you alone are God.

When I remember your character and love for me, I am renewed in my calling. You stand faithfully over all creation. You never grow weak or weary. You never want to quit or resign like I do. During these few short hours of sleep, please replenish my heart with your love and power to be the mother you are calling me to be. And if by your grace I awake in the morning, help me rest in your minute-by-minute provisions instead of seeking to be self-reliant.

Have you never heard? Have you never understood? The LORD is the everlasting God, the Creator of all the earth. He never grows weak or weary. No one can measure the depths of his understanding. ISAIAH 40:28

☼ A prayer about EMPATHY
When I need to balance compassion with motivation

GOD,

When I talk with my children about the Golden Rule, it's usually in reference to treating others kindly. But the principle of doing to others as we would like them to do to us also applies to motivating them when they need a boost. Please give me wisdom to empathize with how my kids are feeling, as well as wisdom to know when they need a nudge out of self-pity. When they're stuck wallowing in the doldrums, give me tact to speak truth, even when it may first seem as if I'm being unsympathetic.

I have been on the receiving end of that kind of love in action, and although someone's realistic words didn't give me the luxury to mope, I appreciated being dealt with honestly. I also grew to see myself as stronger than I had thought. I want to give that gentle honesty to my family as well. Every now and then, we all need the gift of hope beyond a present disappointment. Thank you, Lord, for not seeing us as victims, but as victors in you. I'm grateful that you empathize with my feelings, all the while inspiring me to move beyond them.

Do to others whatever you would like them to do to you.
MATTHEW 7:12

☼ A prayer about SELFISHNESS
When I need to put my husband's needs before my own

LORD,

"One hope—one vision." That was certainly our outlook when my husband and I were first married. But the sweet unity we once enjoyed has now been eroded by division and discord. Today our home and marriage seem divided. Usually I want to pursue my own way and refuse to see the merits of his way. My needs seem to be supreme and trump all other requests.

Lord, forgive my selfish heart. Help me to put away my childish behavior and replace my self-centered desires with others-centered ones. Grant me meekness and humility as I deal with my husband. Give me opportunities to put his needs before my own this week. Show me the right words to communicate that he is precious and the love of my life. Dear Lord, you communicated your love to me by putting my needs before your own comfort as you went to the Cross. Your death in my place motivates me to die to my self-seeking plans. Give me passion to love my husband in an unconditional and self-sacrificing way.

Don't be selfish; don't try to impress others. Be humble, thinking of others as better than yourselves.
PHILIPPIANS 2:3

☀ A prayer about CRISIS
When I dread the next upheaval

GOD,

Dreading the future is no way to live, but that's been my norm lately. One or two crises have me on full alert for the next ball to drop. If only I could truly relax. If only I could get a breather. Lord, I don't want to be driven by fear, but I can't see the future. I can't know how to prepare for trouble that I can't see coming. Even so, I want to live in peace that comes from believing you've got us covered in good times and bad.

My limited vision can be twenty-twenty spiritual sight from your perspective, though, because it can sharpen the eyes of my faith in you. It can turn me to you for guidance. It can keep me seeking your Spirit to continually prepare me. Please ready me exactly as you know I'll need to be for today and tomorrow, too. Work behind the scenes to provide what my family and I will need when trouble comes. Let my sureness in you bless others when they face crises, and inspire my children to live with faith. Steady me with yourself so that I can steady others.

[Jesus] replied, "The Father alone has the authority to set those dates and times, and they are not for you to know. But you will receive power when the Holy Spirit comes upon you." ACTS 1:7-8

☼ A prayer about PRIORITIES
When I need to learn to say no

FATHER,

As I scan my smartphone, I am convicted by my failure to say no. My calendar is filled to overflowing with many good activities and interests but not many strategic opportunities. My e-mail beckons me to respond to the continual requests for my time, effort, and energies. My voice mail reminds me of calls I've missed and relationships that could use some attention. My wallet and receipts are another matter entirely. I hold evidences of purchases made on a whim with little or no thought to our family budget.

I admit, Father, that fear is at the root of many of these poor decisions. I fear letting others down. I fear what saying no might do to my reputation as a capable person. I fear how ceasing from activity and sitting in silence might cause me to have to examine my own heart. Besides the fear, I think an element of misunderstanding is also there. My confusion lies in the fact that I practically live as though the many priorities in my life compete with one another. Thank you, Father, for showing me in the busyness of today that I have not many priorities but only one. You are my singular priority, and everything else flows from keeping that priority preeminent.

Be careful how you live. Don't live like fools, but like those who are wise. EPHESIANS 5:15

☀ **A prayer about GOSSIP**
   When I need to remember to close my mouth

LOVING FATHER,

Lately I've noticed that when I'm talking with other mothers, it is all too easy to get caught up in petty gossip. I like to be included in the lives and interests of my friends, but that can get me into trouble. Help me to discern when to butt out and mind my own business. Remind me that everything that comes out of my mouth should build others up and not tear them down.

Let us aim for harmony in the church and try to build each other up. ROMANS 14:19

DAY 273 *Prayerful Moment*

☀ **A prayer about FAITH**
   When I need you to boost my trust

FATHER,

As I consider what lies ahead of me, I get nervous. I'm not sure my faith is even as big as a mustard seed. Even so, will you meet me there, at that meager place? Thank you that I don't have to have it all together to gain your attention. I give you what I have. Please grow me from here.

The Lord answered, "If you had faith even as small as a mustard seed, you could say to this mulberry tree, 'May you be uprooted and thrown into the sea,' and it would obey you!" LUKE 17:6

☀ A prayer about TRANSFORMATION
When I need to change my perspective

GOD,

I am confused and overwhelmed by the enormity of the task of parenting. It seems especially daunting because I do not fit the role of a traditional mother as I pursue a career outside the home. I feel the conforming pressures of the world dictating to me how a good mother should look and act. At times I am jealous, and I crave the approval of others who labor from home. I need wisdom and discernment to follow your prescribed will for my life, Lord.

Please give me courage to leave the superficial mold behind. Convict me of areas where I am seeking to please others more than you. I want to lay aside the masks I wear to impress others. I need something far superior to a quick fix. Transform my heart to bring it in line with yours. I desire to look more like you than what I perceive the world thinks I should look like. I want to think your thoughts today about this high and holy calling—motherhood.

Don't copy the behavior and customs of this world, but let God transform you into a new person by changing the way you think. Then you will learn to know God's will for you, which is good and pleasing and perfect. ROMANS 12:2

※ **A prayer about ANGER**
When I need to stand up to someone's ire

FATHER,

Someone verbally attacked my child. Angry, unkind words melted his young face; shame and hurt shadowed his eyes; and I know he wondered, *Did I really deserve that?* This wasn't the first time someone showed anger toward my offspring. Sometimes I have no problem speaking up in my child's defense. He needs to know I will not stand for someone treating him badly.

However, sometimes my response lodges in my mouth, and I have trouble knowing what to say. You see, Lord, another person's anger can be intimidating to me, too. When that person has influence in my own life, I trip over my convictions and I wonder how strongly to speak up, or if I should at all because of the potential backlash. I'm ashamed to admit that there have been times when I did not assert myself enough on my children's behalf or my own. I need courage to face bullies as much as my kids do. Please give me wise boldness and confident tact to show my children that they are worth defending. Please help me to be reliable as a place of safety and justice for them.

A hot-tempered person starts fights; a cool-tempered person stops them. . . . It is wonderful to say the right thing at the right time! PROVERBS 15:18, 23

☀ A prayer about GENEROSITY
When I need to check my spirit

HEAVENLY FATHER,

Being a mother, I feel like I give and give all the time. I pour out my time, energy, love, and service over and over every day. I do this because I love my family, but so many times I find myself feeling resentful. I fall into the trap of feeling it isn't fair that I sacrifice so much of myself and seem to get so little in return. I need you to remind me that this is not the truth. This is a lie that Satan wants me to believe.

Help me remember that I am truly blessed. Expand my heart so that I give generously to all of your children without expecting reciprocation. Remind me of the countless ways you have provided for me today, and give me your peace.

If you give even a cup of cold water to one of the least of my followers, you will surely be rewarded. MATTHEW 10:42

☼ A prayer about SURRENDER
When my loyalties are divided

HEAVENLY FATHER,

I confess I have been withholding parts of my life from you. I can so easily fall into wrong thinking when I examine how my faith and life interrelate. Even though I know that all of life should be considered sacred, I often display many secular attitudes.

But today is a new beginning and a chance to examine my heart before you. As I take inventory, I repent of anything that is less than total surrender. I offer my whole body, mind, and soul to you, Lord. Here are my hands to serve you and others. I give you my feet to seek to walk in your ways. I offer my eyes and ask you to change my perspective to match yours. And Father, my mind belongs to you. Please align my thoughts according to your Word and wisdom. I give you my *whole* heart this time, Lord. Conform my affections to reflect the desires of your heart and help me live a life of unconditional surrender to your will.

Dear brothers and sisters, I plead with you to give your bodies to God because of all he has done for you. Let them be a living and holy sacrifice—the kind he will find acceptable. This is truly the way to worship him. ROMANS 12:1

☀ A prayer about APPRECIATION
When I forget to thank you

GOD,

It's said that the little things are the big things, and nowhere can that be more true than when it comes to feeling appreciated. Some days it seems that my role as mother is taken for granted. If only my kids knew how often I think of them throughout each day. If only my family would think more often of the little ways I keep our household going. If only . . . Can you tell I'm not feeling very appreciated lately, God? But as I gripe about my undervalued existence, you halt my complaints and clarify that the faulty habit may not be just my family's. So Lord, here are a few reasons *I* appreciate *you* and this life you've blessed me with:

1. My precious and sometimes frustrating family who bless and challenge me
2. Your consistency in so many ways that keeps me going—and that I often overlook
3. Your gentle lessons that help me grow

For these and so much more, Lord, I thank you.

May the LORD bless you and protect you. May the LORD smile on you and be gracious to you. May the LORD show you his favor and give you his peace. NUMBERS 6:24-26

☼ **A prayer about REVERENCE**
When I need to stand in awe

FATHER GOD,
My daily routine seems to make me oblivious to your presence. But how can I be so indifferent and unmoved by your profound and creative works? When I see the sky stained red and orange around the rising sun, or when I watch the birds darting at the feeder, I have to stop for a moment to marvel at your handiwork. Too often, though, my heart is numb to the splendor of your awesome deeds. Change my apathetic heart and awaken my spirit to stand in awe of who you are—and then shout for joy.

Those who live at the ends of the earth stand in awe of your wonders. From where the sun rises to where it sets, you inspire shouts of joy. PSALM 65:8

☼ **A prayer about REGRETS**
When I fear making long-lasting mistakes

GOD,
When my child is grown, I don't want to look back and have regrets about the way I raised him. I need your wisdom in my parenting decisions today. I want to discover your will in my life and teach my child to follow you as well. I know you have good plans for our lives and I trust you.

Let the message about Christ, in all its richness, fill your lives. Teach and counsel each other with all the wisdom he gives.
COLOSSIANS 3:16

✿ **A prayer about HURTS**
When I need to deal with my past

LORD,

I have been through a number of painful experiences, each of which has left a scar on my heart and could affect the way I parent my child. I don't want to pass along the wounds of my past to my own child. I want to be able to acknowledge the wounds, learn what I can from them, and then leave them in the past. But sometimes that is easier said than done. It is much more comfortable to stuff down the pain and avoid dealing with the aftermath that comes from facing my issues.

Help me to find the courage to face my past. Walk with me as I heal and grow into a more whole mother. As I identify areas where I have been wounded, help me turn them over to you. Help me to show my child how to love and trust you with her life and leave her a legacy of hope.

Choose today whom you will serve. . . . As for me and my family, we will serve the LORD. JOSHUA 24:15

☼ A prayer about MOVING
When I am scared of change

LORD JESUS,

As we prepare for a new adventure, I am both excited and anxious. Moving to a new place requires finding a new place to belong. I want my children to feel safe and secure in the midst of the upheaval. But this is not something I can control. Thank you for always promising to be with us, no matter where we live. You go before us and prepare a place for us. You know exactly how we will fit into this new chapter of life, and you will walk with us every step of the way. Help me to trust in you and allow you to calm my fears. Help my children adjust quickly and thrive in their new environment. Help me to walk confidently with you into this new stage of life. Guide us in the right path so we can grow closer to you.

You know my thoughts even when I'm far away. You see me when I travel and when I rest at home. You know everything I do. You know what I am going to say even before I say it, LORD. You go before me and follow me. You place your hand of blessing on my head. Such knowledge is too wonderful for me, too great for me to understand! I can never escape from your Spirit! I can never get away from your presence!

PSALM 139:2-7

☼ A prayer about BITTERNESS
When I feel the seed of resentment grow

LORD,

I need your heart surgery. This negative feeling I've had isn't going away. In fact, it's growing instead of fading, and I'm weary of feeling resentful. It's turning into outright bitterness, and that scares me. I don't want to be poisoned by an unhealthy spirit, and I don't want my family to be corrupted by it either. But God, this problem is obviously too big for me to correct on my own, or it wouldn't still be an issue. I'm ready for you to do what's needed to heal and re-create me from the inside out. Please loosen any remaining grip I have on this grudge. Help me let go and move beyond to a place of forgiveness and peace that you offer. In fact, God, please do such a work in me that others are inspired to give you their hearts as well.

Thank you for the wholeness I trust you are working into me even now. I also trust that you will hold me through the cleaning out of my heart. It may sting, but I will be stronger and more like you because of it.

Look after each other so that none of you fails to receive the grace of God. Watch out that no poisonous root of bitterness grows up to trouble you, corrupting many.
HEBREWS 12:15

DAY 284

☼ A prayer about GOD'S TIMING
When I am impatient with his plan

LORD,

You know I am getting impatient and frustrated as I wait
to hear about whether or not my husband is getting a new
job. We have tried to pray daily for this big decision. God,
you are all-knowing and gracious, but at times receiving
a "wait on me" response from you can be tough. Some
days I allow fear to creep in, as this potential job change
will have a huge impact on our family. Please help me rest
firmly in your will for us. You hold our present and our
future in your hands.

Settle my heart, I pray, and give me strength to wait
and see if you will open or close the door. I know that both
anxiety and faith are contagious. Help me model steadfast
trust to my family, reminding them of your constant care.
Lord, your timing is perfect, and your plans are flawless.
We wait expectantly for your good direction.

*You must not forget this one thing, dear friends: A day is
like a thousand years to the Lord, and a thousand years is
like a day.* 2 PETER 3:8

⚙ **A prayer about FINANCES**
   When I need to change my focus

LORD GOD,

Money is tight right now, so I find myself thinking about it more than I should. I worry about not having enough and am tempted to chase after that elusive security that is always just out of reach. I wish I could live life without money, but this is impossible. Until I get to heaven, then, I will need to figure out a healthy way to deal with money without letting it get a grip on me.

You have promised to take care of my needs if I only give my worries to you. I want to trust you completely, so please help me to let go of my fear that you will not take care of me. Help me to trust you with my resources and allow you to guide my decisions about how I should use my money. Help me to worship you and to find my security in you alone.

This same God who takes care of me will supply all your needs from his glorious riches, which have been given to us in Christ Jesus. PHILIPPIANS 4:19

⚙ **A prayer about FAITHFULNESS**
When I praise you for holding my children's future

LORD,

You promise to be faithful. Help my children to understand that your faithfulness is specifically for them, too. You love them even more than I do, and I trust you to work as needed in them. Soften their hearts to you, and help them desire you above all else.

I will be your God throughout your lifetime—until your hair is white with age. I made you, and I will care for you. I will carry you along and save you. ISAIAH 46:4

DAY 287 *Prayerful Moment*

⚙ **A prayer about STRENGTH**
When I am weary and depleted

FATHER,

I am spiritually and physically depleted. I have exhausted all my human resources. This is exactly where you have led me, to be totally dependent on you. You are my source of strength. You alone will give me the power and perseverance to do everything you have called me to do today. Thank you, Lord.

I can do everything through Christ, who gives me strength.
PHILIPPIANS 4:13

☼ **A prayer about FREEDOM**
When I need to let go of trying to be perfect

LORD,

Life is much easier with a list of rules. A checklist in black and white allows me to rate myself. Of course, when I fall short I beat myself up. You have invited me to live a life of freedom from rules—a life that is about relationship rather than living up to an impossible standard. It sounds so easy but has proven to be so difficult to put into practice.

Teach me how to stop checking off the lists of "shoulds" and "should nots" and focus on living a life that is pleasing to you. Help me to understand what true freedom looks like and to seek to follow your will daily. Thank you for giving me the choice to follow you every day and for crediting Christ's righteousness and holiness to me.

Jesus said to the people who believed in him, "You are truly my disciples if you remain faithful to my teachings. And you will know the truth, and the truth will set you free."
JOHN 8:31-32

☀ A prayer about DIVORCE
When my kids struggle to find their way through it

FATHER,

It sounds trite from a human level, but when all else fails and relationships crumble, your love really is the answer. There's a lot involved in that healing love; it isn't merely a fluffy, feel-good emotion that swoops down to plaster smiles on our faces. Your love is the only true love, and we're counting on it even now. Although it's not your way, and it certainly wasn't the plan at the wedding, divorce sometimes happens. Too often, actually. And it just hurts and hurts some more. Even when there's no other safe way to function and divorce seems inevitable, it is still painful, because you created us for unity.

God, you must grieve, especially for the young ones who flounder through the demolition of a family. They're already vulnerable and feeling caught in the middle, and then to add this to their pressures . . . When will the heartbreak end and real love take over? Please, Lord, overflow us with your unifying love. Your love is what will heal our hearts and lives, even if living together again doesn't happen. Draw us together with a spirit of forgiveness so we can experience what healing love can do.

Above all, clothe yourselves with love, which binds us all together in perfect harmony. COLOSSIANS 3:14

☀ A prayer about SENSITIVITY
When I stand in judgment of others

FATHER,

I confess that I am far too quick to judge other people's choices and decisions. Sometimes the issue is how they choose to discipline their children. Other times it's what they allow their children to watch or listen to. This gets complicated and especially challenging when our children are playmates.

Please help me, Lord, to believe the best of other parents' motivations and intentions. I know that in many areas Scripture does not clearly prohibit certain behaviors. Help me to not add a word to your holy Word. Where you allow freedom, I pray that I would truly experience freedom. Father, I admit that in some of my relationships I can be ungracious in my words and actions. Bring reconciliation in those times of offense. Please bring repentance where I have stood in judgment over others. Let me show consideration and grace to the other parents in my life.

We who are strong must be considerate of those who are sensitive about things like this. We must not just please ourselves. ROMANS 15:1

☼ A prayer about CONFIDENCE
When I see my child's insecurity

JESUS,

Oh, how this part of parenting hurts! When insecurity flares in my child and he struggles to feel good enough, my heart aches. I understand insecurity; I've been there. And if shaky confidence weren't rough enough on its own, it's usually compounded by shame and frustration over hiding that tenderness from others. Insecure people often get stomped on in our slam-dunk, reach-the-finish-line-first society.

But Jesus, you never have asked us to prove ourselves. You don't define worth or strength the way the rest of us often do. Instead, as you walked this earth, you showed us what steady confidence looks like and where its source of strength lies. You, Jesus, are my child's helper. I'm so relieved by that fact. Please show him that he is okay because he's yours. Please give him early and consistent victories in choosing to find his worth in you while shutting his eyes and ears to the world's mixed messages about him. The world is not out for his best, but you are. Thank you for loving him so much, Lord. Please fill him with confidence because of who he is in you.

We can say with confidence, "The LORD is my helper, so I will have no fear. What can mere people do to me?"
HEBREWS 13:6

☼ A prayer about THOUGHTS
When I want to align my thinking to God's Word

GOD,

As a mother, I have many goals and purposes for my children. The goal that I been the most passionate about for many years is helping them think biblically about all of life. Your thoughts are precious, and we long as a family to reflect them to others. You are our King who rules and reigns over all creation. Every single inch of this entire world belongs to you.

Train my daughter to think biblically about the arts. Please show my son how to solve problems for your glory. Saturate our daily walk with your Word. Discipline our minds to take every thought captive and examine where they don't align with what pleases you. Bring into line our thinking with your truth. Help us to forsake worldly ideas and to examine ungodly worldviews that have contaminated our beliefs. We want our lives individually and corporately as a family to glorify you. We repent of our double-minded ways. Replace our doubts with the beauty of your truth. Replace our unprofitable ideas with a passion for your truth.

May all my thoughts be pleasing to him, for I rejoice in the LORD. PSALM 104:34

☼ A prayer about PERSPECTIVE
When I need a reminder of how God sees me

HEAVENLY FATHER,

Today I am reveling in the fact that I am your child, your precious daughter. You have chosen me as your own. You died for my sins and invited me to live life with you. Thank you for loving me. Let me live today in the joy that comes from knowing that I am yours forever.

Listen to me, O royal daughter; take to heart what I say. Forget your people and your family far away. For your royal husband delights in your beauty; honor him, for he is your lord.
PSALM 45:10-11

☼ A prayer about AVAILABILITY
When I need to wait in the wings

LORD,

Practicing quiet availability is an art, especially as a mother. My instincts say, *Get involved, give my two cents' worth. I'm the mother; they need my advice, right?* But you quiet my intervening nature with the reminder that as my children grow up, they need to bear more responsibility and make more of their own decisions. It wouldn't be healthy for them to need me 24/7 anymore. Help me to remain quietly available until they request my input. Thank you for your sensitive example of that art.

Be quick to listen, slow to speak. JAMES 1:19

☼ **A prayer about CHALLENGES**
When I feel like giving up

LORD,

I'm not typically one to cave under pressure. In fact, I pride myself on rolling with the punches, on my ability to keep on keeping on. But this time I wonder how I'll continue facing this challenge. I'm beyond worn out; I reached worn out several seasons ago, but here I still find myself, desperate for you to change something.

Will you please do for me what Psalm 28:7 says? Be my strength and shield. Help me trust you with *all* my heart, particularly the chunk of it that has become complacent with doubting you. I need your help now; I need the joy that comes from knowing you're with me through this, that you have more for me beyond this. One more time, here is my sacrifice of thanksgiving in a season that threatens to make me give up. Today gratitude indeed feels costly. But you deserve it, and I trust that you will help me desire the deeper gifts you offer when I lay my last strength at your throne. Thank you again, Father, for not quitting on me.

The LORD is my strength and shield. I trust him with all my heart. He helps me, and my heart is filled with joy. I burst out in songs of thanksgiving. PSALM 28:7

⚛ A prayer about CONTROL
When I find myself pushing too hard

FATHER,

I have so many dreams for my children. Having hopes for the future is not wrong, but it becomes detrimental if I force my desires on my children instead of letting them become their own people.

Help me to temper my tendency to try to control my kids' lives. Teach me how to hold my children with open hands. I give my children's future over to you and ask you to form them into healthy, happy adults. Help me to discover and nurture the talents and gifts you have given my children so they can use them for your purposes. Teach me how to inspire my children to be the best they can be without pushing them into becoming something I want them to be. Remind me that you have their future in your hands.

Trust in the LORD with all your heart; do not depend on your own understanding. Seek his will in all you do, and he will show you which path to take. PROVERBS 3:5-6

☸ A prayer about CONFRONTATION
When I dread a brewing battle

LORD,

Here we go again. I feel another battle brewing, which means another inevitable confrontation. I think the trepidation ahead of time is as bad as the blowup itself. I want to work toward peace, as far as it's up to me. But I can't back down on some things, Father, and I need your wisdom to know when to put my foot down and when to let it go. Please bathe this situation in your Spirit of peace and harmony. Help us be united to work toward the best solution that honors you and respects each other.

When we meet at the Cross, we can work through anything, right? Thanks for going before us and for guiding us through our differences. Please keep the vision in front of us of greater growth and a richer relationship because of the work we put in. But Lord, in case I don't receive the care and respect I hope to give, please be my defender and help me trust you to guard my reputation and my hopes.

Work at living in peace with everyone, and work at living a holy life, for those who are not holy will not see the Lord.
HEBREWS 12:14

❁ A prayer about SERVICE
When I need the help of the Good Shepherd

JESUS,

Thank you for the little lambs you have entrusted to my care. They are such a source of great joy. Thank you for the chance to partner with you in meeting their needs, large and small. Whether it means feeding them or guiding them into safer pastures, this is a sacred calling. I am grateful that you have given each of my children to me, and I desire to be intimately involved in their protection and well-being. What a blessing to see them thrive!

You, Lord, were the Lamb that was slaughtered to provide a way of rescue for us. You willingly laid down your life for the sheep. You protect your little ones from harm. These acts of selfless love and care motivate me to give and give a little more. I need courage and resolve to shepherd my children and their hearts. Please curb my wayward impulses and refuel my soul to serve another day.

Care for the flock that God has entrusted to you. Watch over it willingly, not grudgingly—not for what you will get out of it, but because you are eager to serve God. 1 PETER 5:2

☀ A prayer about SPIRITUAL WARFARE
When I need a battle mentality

LORD,

Awake my sleepy soul to the realization that I live in a war zone. Often I parent with a peacetime mentality, and I can be naive and casual as I interact with the surrounding culture. The world is really a battleground for my children's souls. You, God, have given us not only the warning but also the provision of your protection. Guard our minds with the helmet of salvation. Protect our hearts with the breastplate of righteousness. Prepare our feet for the gospel battle. Teach us what it means to courageously take up the shield of faith. Thank you for the sword of the Spirit. We long to be a light for you in this dark world.

Because I am a mother, you have given me the task of spiritually preparing my children to engage with the world. Please give them grace, dear Lord, to be in the world but not of it. Shelter them from the evil one and his lies and schemes. Give them victory through the strength that you provide.

Put on every piece of God's armor so you will be able to resist the enemy in the time of evil. Then after the battle you will still be standing firm. EPHESIANS 6:13

☼ A prayer about COMFORT
When I hope to model prioritizing others' needs

HEAVENLY FATHER,

Thank you for caring about each need on this earth. The heartaches are too many for me to comprehend, but you hurt over every one of them. Please help me to live in a way that encourages my kids to reach out with giving, comforting hearts. Please grow bold tenderness in us to help others in need.

Those who shut their ears to the cries of the poor will be ignored in their own time of need. PROVERBS 21:13

DAY 301 *Prayerful Moment*

☼ A prayer about HOME
When I want my home to be a refuge

LORD,

Soggy cereal on the kitchen floor, upended blocks on the coffee table, backpacks strewn along the hallway—will our home ever be clean for more than ten minutes? When I'm tempted to blow up over the messes my kids make, please remind me that you gave us our home, not to be a showcase that impresses guests, but to be the place where our family can love, laugh, and grow together. As I teach my kids to pick up after themselves, may I model the same patience and understanding you show me as I strive to clean up my own heart.

A wise woman builds her home, but a foolish woman tears it down with her own hands. PROVERBS 14:1

☼ A prayer about APPEARANCE
When I wish to feel more attractive

LORD,

I'm not having a great hair day. I'm not exactly a fashionista today either, with these old shoes and this outfit that has seen better days. And my figure—I'm nearly sure I remember it being better, long ago. I almost remember the days when I had time to linger on my appearance. The fact is, since becoming a mother, my mind is first on my family. My heart wants their good first, which means most times they get my primary attention. But I haven't completely lost the old me, the part that still needs to feel feminine and attractive. You never asked me to give that up. After all, you made me to reflect yourself, and you embody true beauty.

Thank you that I can wear the beauty of your Spirit no matter how little time I have to make myself up each day. Help me to clothe myself with the timeless, ageless treasures of mercy, kindness, humility, gentleness, and patience. I've seen others wear those qualities like fine silks, and they really are the most gorgeous women. Not only do those qualities bless others, but they surely must feel lovely on.

Since God chose you to be the holy people he loves, you must clothe yourselves with tenderhearted mercy, kindness, humility, gentleness, and patience. COLOSSIANS 3:12

⚙ **A prayer about MODESTY**
When I need help guiding my children

FATHER GOD,

As I look around me, I see that young people seem to give less and less care to modesty. Then I hear of the prevalence of sexting and how young girls and boys are sending inappropriate pictures of themselves. I know that this is not pleasing to you and it causes harm to the young people involved.

Help me to teach my children to respect their bodies and to be aware of the message they are sending by the way they choose to dress. Help me to model the values of modesty and inner beauty. Let your light shine through my life. Guard my heart as well as my children's hearts from immoral influences. Help me to appropriately monitor what they are seeing through the media that enters my home.

Don't be concerned about the outward beauty of fancy hairstyles, expensive jewelry, or beautiful clothes. You should clothe yourselves instead with the beauty that comes from within, the unfading beauty of a gentle and quiet spirit, which is so precious to God. I PETER 3:3-4

☀ A prayer about BELONGING
When I want to share the joy of being yours

LORD,

The human need to belong is so powerful. I think of children who grow up in unstable homes or who get shuffled from one foster-care situation to another, never enjoying the sureness of belonging to anyone who truly loves them. A lack of healthy belonging ensures brokenness. This world does not nurture eternal belonging. Sin has warped it and continues its insidious work of tearing apart bonds that were created to remain intact, offering wholeness and security. You created human beings to connect at the deepest levels with you and each other. But that goodness has been broken in so many ways for so many people.

Lord, you see those who need to belong to you. You see the ones who do but need to be reminded of that sure attachment. Show them in a personal way that you died so they could be yours once more. Heal and rebuild as only you can. And Lord, may my lifestyle of faith and joy invite my children and others into an eternal, life-giving attachment to you.

You are a chosen people. You are royal priests, a holy nation, God's very own possession. As a result, you can show others the goodness of God, for he called you out of the darkness into his wonderful light. I PETER 2:9

☀ **A prayer about INTEGRITY**
 When I want to instill values in my children

LORD,

I want to be able to be a good role model for my children. But, as you know, I am not perfect; I need your correction and guidance every day. I sometimes forget that although it can be easy to justify a little white lie, my children are watching me and taking their cues from me.

Help me to remember that, in every situation, truth and integrity are always the best way to go. Stop me mid-sentence when I am stretching the truth or choosing what seems to be the easier path of deception. Enable me to learn what it means to speak with grace and truth, as you do. Grow in me the fruit of your Spirit so that I can instill truth-telling in my children. Thank you for modeling honesty, and help me to be more like you every day.

The LORD detests lying lips, but he delights in those who tell the truth. PROVERBS 12:22

☀ A prayer about GOODNESS
When this life brings me down

HEAVENLY FATHER,

War, hurricanes, raging fires, senseless acts of violence—the fallen world around me can cause me to doubt whether goodness actually exists anymore. There are days when I find myself dwelling too much on the negativity and pain around me.

But I need only to look into the laughing face of my child at play to remember that ultimately we were all created in your image and that you indeed are good. This world is not an accurate reflection of your character. Remind me every day that my stay here in this corrupted world is temporary and that you have prepared a place for me filled with joy and peace. Show me how I can manifest your character today in all of my interactions—to bring a tangible piece of you to the world around me.

Surely your goodness and unfailing love will pursue me all the days of my life, and I will live in the house of the LORD forever. PSALM 23:6

☼ **A prayer about FORGIVENESS**
  When I realize I am still bitter

LORD,

Just when I thought I had mastered forgiveness, one small reminder of a past hurt has brought back all my old resentment and anger. Please change my heart and help me to give this burden to you again. Flood my soul with your mercy so that I can truly change.

Be kind to each other, tenderhearted, forgiving one another, just as God through Christ has forgiven you.
EPHESIANS 4:32

DAY 308 *Prayerful Moment*

☼ **A prayer about OBEDIENCE**
  When I need patience

MY FATHER,

Give me your strength today as my child is testing me. Help me to keep my temper and use this disobedience as a teaching moment, even when I want to lash out in anger. Help me display the fruit of your Spirit, particularly patience, gentleness, kindness, and self-control.

Children, obey your parents because you belong to the Lord, for this is the right thing to do. . . . Fathers, do not provoke your children to anger by the way you treat them. Rather, bring them up with the discipline and instruction that comes from the Lord. EPHESIANS 6:1, 4

⚙ **A prayer about PRAYER**
When I need to speak to God

LORD,

I feel as though I am drowning in despair today. I am struggling to see how trials, hope, and prayer can go together in this moment. I cannot rejoice in my test, but please show me, Lord, how to rejoice in the hope that only you can give. Help me to rest in the knowledge that my hope does not lie in the changing of my circumstances but rather in my reliance on you.

Lord, my desire is for things to be resolved immediately. But I know you are calling me to be patient and to persevere in this trouble. Help me to abide in you and remain in you regardless of how long this trial lasts. Help me not only to persevere in this trial but to persevere in prayer, bringing all my questions, anxieties, and requests to you. I am so thankful that I can come to you in prayer any moment of any day.

Rejoice in our confident hope. Be patient in trouble, and keep on praying. ROMANS 12:12

☀ **A prayer about SIMPLICITY**
When I try to complicate matters

FATHER,

The older I get, the more I crave simplicity. Life decisions and time management can be so complex. Relationships can also get tricky and sometimes be problematic. Commitments to roles and responsibilities can oftentimes seem eternal, and even the daily tasks that lie before me can seem daunting. Help me, dear Father, to strip life down to the basics and the things that really count.

You have reminded us that life is ultimately about loving you and loving others. So why am I so often tempted to think that through addition of material things and accomplishments life will actually be more? Show me how, in reality, less can be more. This is the pattern you designed for my life to flourish and prosper. Give me the discernment to say no to good things and yes to the *best* things. I want wisdom and courage to make the choices necessary for living a simpler life.

[Jesus said,] "My yoke is easy to bear, and the burden I give you is light." MATTHEW 11:30

🌼 **A prayer about DOUBT**
When it robs me of the Spirit's fullness

LORD,

Sometimes when I'm stuck in doubt I forget the blessings reserved for those who take you at your word. Those blessings are a big motivation for tossing off failing faith and putting all my trust in you. I want to trust you wholly and not miss out on your best. That means not giving time to doubts that hinder the fullness of what you'd like to do in and through me. Sounds easy, but the humanness in me likes to complicate things.

When my heart wants more answers to my questions and I wonder if you'll come through again and on time, please whisper to me a reminder of the blessed path of resisting doubt. If I don't listen well at first, please shout as loudly as necessary to get my attention. Remind me that you never doubt yourself and that your Spirit in me can help me live with faith. Thank you for the blessings to come.

Jesus told him, "You believe because you have seen me. Blessed are those who believe without seeing me."
JOHN 20:29

☼ A prayer about VULNERABILITY
When I am afraid to be transparent

PRECIOUS LORD,

Today has been filled with frustrations and disappointments. I want to run and hide somewhere far, far away. I know that if I run to the heights, you are there. If I try to escape to the depths, you are there. You see all and know all. Most amazing is that you have examined the recesses of my heart and know everything about me; yet somehow you still love me. I am overwhelmed by your unconditional love for me. I am so undeserving and yet so grateful for this tender care.

As I live in community with others, please give me boldness to be as transparent with my friends as I seek to be with you. Truly sharing from the heart always brings the risk of rejection and being misunderstood. I confess that what keeps me from sharing my true feelings with you or others is fear. Both the fear of people's rejection and the fear of failure can utterly paralyze me. Remind me daily that your perfect love casts out all fear.

O LORD, you have examined my heart and know everything about me. PSALM 139:1

☀ A prayer about PRAISE
When my heart is inspired to worship

FATHER,

Today as I walk through the beauty of your creation, I am overcome by all your goodness to me. You have filled my heart to overflowing with thankfulness for all you have given to my family and me—breath, life, and good gifts too many to count. As I worship you today, I am also convicted by my thanklessness and ingratitude so many other times. I can be quick to see all the things I do not have rather than the many good things I do possess.

Father, please give me a resolve to honor you at all times, not just sometimes. May the first thing on my lips be praise to you rather than praise of myself. Cleanse my heart and mouth of anything that is not praiseworthy. Replace my complaints with words that worship and praise you. May the words of my mouth and the reflections of my heart be contagious to my family and friends. Let the praise of your name fill our home.

I will praise the LORD at all times. I will constantly speak his praises. PSALM 34:1

☼ **A prayer about FATIGUE**
When weariness doesn't let up

LORD,

It's been hard to get up in the mornings lately. My fatigue feels like it goes to my core, dragging down every cell. Please help me to rest in the stillness of your Spirit while you renew my strength even now. Be all I need today, as you have promised, so I can meet my family's needs.

The LORD is my shepherd; I have all that I need. He lets me rest in green meadows; he leads me beside peaceful streams. He renews my strength. PSALM 23:1-3

DAY 315 *Prayerful Moment*

☼ **A prayer about COMPLACENCY**
When status quo distorts my vision

LORD,

Thank you for defining what's right and real despite what the world calls normal. It's so easy just to go along with the fads and fancies of our world. Yet going with the status quo without pausing to question whether it's your way is a sure road to disaster. Please don't let me settle for what isn't really the truth. Give me discernment today so I can make wise choices.

A time is coming when people will no longer listen to sound and wholesome teaching. They will follow their own desires and will look for teachers who will tell them whatever their itching ears want to hear. 2 TIMOTHY 4:3

DAY 316

🔆 A prayer about BALANCE
When I sense my family is overscheduled

FATHER,

Here we go again. A dash to the grocery store before music lessons, before soccer practice, before we speed home so I can toss supper together and the kids can rush through their homework. These activities are good things, some of them even necessary. We have to eat. My kids need to grow as well-rounded people.

But Lord, something in my spirit keeps telling me that part of being well rounded also includes practicing balance. Please help me to model and encourage balanced living. As I'm helping my kids with activities and academics, help me to initiate the occasional lesson of "addition by subtraction." Show me when it's necessary to reduce something good to add to what's best. That's a tough value to live by in today's society. But please help us to prioritize family togetherness, simply being at home with each other. Please impress on us the futility of too much busyness. Father, more than anything, I want to give my children the best life possible. Help me to subtract anything that steals the richness of living close to you and loving each other daily.

We are merely moving shadows, and all our busy rushing ends in nothing. We heap up wealth, not knowing who will spend it. And so, Lord, where do I put my hope? My only hope is in you. PSALM 39:6-7

☼ A prayer about BLESSINGS
When I feel guilty for having so much

LORD,

I suppose that I have something along the lines of survivor's guilt. I look around at my life and feel overwhelmed by the blessings. You've been so good to me. But each day as I enjoy security and love and friends and family and living in wealth compared to most of the world, I struggle with questions of why. Why me? Why do I have so much when so many souls you love equally live in constant crisis? If it isn't war tearing apart lives, it's famine, dirty water, extreme poverty, persecution, crime, and diseases I don't have to fear where I live. And most important, I have been told of your salvation. So many others don't know about that yet.

Please don't let me become complacent or develop a sense of entitlement because of your gifts to me. Otherwise, I'll miss out on the greater gifts of relying on you for everything and having a growing heart that is broken on another's behalf—broken enough to help. Thank you for giving to me so that I can bless others who need a better life on earth and the forever life you offer.

Yes, you will be enriched in every way so that you can always be generous. And when we take your gifts to those who need them, they will thank God. 2 CORINTHIANS 9:11

☀ **A prayer about the BIBLE**
When I want my children to love your Word

GOD,

Psalm 119 is such a great reminder of what your Word means for us. The Bible is readily available in this culture, but how many people go through life missing out on what you say to us in it? I often don't pause to dwell on the fact that you—the Creator and Master of the universe, the eternal Victor and loving Savior—wrote these truths for all humankind, including me. That is truly mind-blowing. At least it is to those who understand who you are.

Father, please help my children to fall in love with you and your messages in your Word. Open the eyes of their hearts, the understanding of their minds, to see why they need to study the Bible. Change their lives through your Word. Make them passionate lovers of you through witnessing how much you love them. Grant them discernment and wisdom to live for you in a world that increasingly despises your ways. Thank you, Lord, for your Word!

I will study your commandments and reflect on your ways. I will delight in your decrees and not forget your word. Be good to your servant, that I may live and obey your word. Open my eyes to see the wonderful truths in your instructions. PSALM 119:15-18

☼ **A prayer about DEPRESSION**
When I need wisdom to know how to help

JESUS,

Thank you for today's Scripture verse. I've been at a loss to know how to help when someone I care about is feeling low. Finding the right balance of what to say, when to listen silently, when to nudge, and when to hold back takes skill and sensitivity beyond my natural abilities. I so want to help instead of adding more burden to someone's already wounded heart.

I love how today's verse points me to you, the one on whom the Holy Spirit rested while you were on earth bringing healing to so many people. You're the one who sent his Spirit to remain on earth to minister to us. On my own, I can't see the big picture like you can. I don't always know what another person needs, so I need you to work in and through me. Please fill me with yourself so that I can share your wisdom and understanding, your counsel and might, and so that I may offer the knowledge and encouragement you know someone else needs. I'm trusting you to help me offer *you*.

The Spirit of the LORD will rest on him—the Spirit of wisdom and understanding, the Spirit of counsel and might, the Spirit of knowledge and the fear of the LORD.
ISAIAH 11:2

☀ A prayer about COMMUNITY
When I need awareness of my role in it

FATHER,

Today's verse isn't usually talked about in reference to community. Typically it's mentioned in discussions about hospitality. Yet it seems to me that it offers a new outlook about my part in the community you've placed me in.

The idea of crossing paths with an angel is surprising. Angels are part of heaven, reminders of you, not of earth. But if I'm looking for your Spirit's presence in each encounter with another person, I can participate in bringing a little heaven to earth. When people sense a welcome from me, surely they'll be touched by your love, right? That experience of sweet grace ought to take many people by surprise because an encounter with your Spirit goes beyond the best comfort this world can boast. Who knows, maybe I can share a taste of your divine nature to enrich this community. Please help me to act as an angel on earth and surprise someone today.

Don't forget to show hospitality to strangers, for some who have done this have entertained angels without realizing it!
HEBREWS 13:2

☼ A prayer about HAPPINESS
When I am satisfied

HEAVENLY FATHER,

I woke up this morning with a light heart. You have certainly showered your blessings on me lately. Simple pleasures like baking and singing with my kids fill me with joy. The memories of these last few weeks already make me smile. I know life will not always be this smooth, but I am so grateful for the harmony in our home right now.

I have learned how to be content with whatever I have.
PHILIPPIANS 4:11

DAY 322 *Prayerful Moment*

☼ A prayer about the PAST
When I need to remember grace

LORD,

I shudder to think of all of the ways I have strayed from your path and disobeyed your commands. I can bog myself down in regret and shame when I remember past mistakes. You have promised me that you have washed me clean and forgiven me. Help me to forgive myself and move forward in the freedom of the new life you have given me. Thank you for the fresh start that you offer me today.

He has removed our sins as far from us as the east is from the west. PSALM 103:12

❀ A prayer about MONEY
When I want to teach my child to share

LORD,

As my child grows, I am mindful of the countless ways you provide for our family. You watch over us and bless us time and again with shelter, food, and other material possessions. I desire to teach my child to be grateful for all the resources you have given her so that she can learn to steward those resources in a way that honors you.

Help me to instill this value into my child. Show me ways I can encourage her to praise you for your many blessings and to share what she has with a pure heart. Thank you for always being faithful to provide what we need.

"Bring all the tithes into the storehouse so there will be enough food in my Temple. If you do," says the LORD of Heaven's Armies, "I will open the windows of heaven for you. I will pour out a blessing so great you won't have enough room to take it in! Try it! Put me to the test!"

MALACHI 3:10

☼ A prayer about DISAPPOINTING OTHERS
When I can't do it all

LORD JESUS,

I had the best of intentions, but I blew it. I made a promise that I wasn't able to keep—time just got away from me. Please help calm my racing thoughts, and remind me that you will hold me up when I fall. Give me the courage to admit my failing promptly. If there is a way to make things up with the person I've wronged, please help me to see it.

From now on, help me to prioritize my time so that I accomplish the things that you have planned for me to do through your strength. Teach me to say no to requests that I'm not meant or able to fulfill. And as horrible as I feel about letting someone down, use this failing to remind me of your grace when others fail to meet my expectations too. Thank you for never giving up on me.

There is no condemnation for those who belong to Christ Jesus. ROMANS 8:1

❄ A prayer about RIGHTEOUSNESS
When I am wrong about being right with God

LORD,

I resign from my tired methodology of trying harder to do better so that you will love me more. It doesn't work and it never will. I will never be good enough or smart enough to acquire your love. I need a righteousness that comes from outside of myself. I need a righteousness that I can never earn or deserve by my good deeds. No amount of self-effort, self-improvement, or self-righteousness is sufficient to merit your grace.

Lord, forgive my crooked ways of trying to make myself right with you. Your righteousness given to me is the only thing that will straighten out my heart and my days. I want to be right in your sight and established in your love. Thank you for the gift of faith that provides the passageway to being rightly related to you. Help me live in such a way that I never doubt that the Cross was necessary and essential for my salvation.

I no longer count on my own righteousness through obeying the law; rather, I become righteous through faith in Christ. For God's way of making us right with himself depends on faith. PHILIPPIANS 3:9

☼ A prayer about SEEKING GOD
When I need to want to know him better

LORD,

Seeking you requires stillness, and listening to you requires silence. Actually drawing closer to know you will require time and effort. Those realities are in short supply right now in our home. But truthfully, I seem to find time to pursue other things, such as leisure, friendships, and personal time.

Please transform my heart, Lord, to give you first place. Transform me into a person who finds enjoyment in seeking you and attempts to make that a priority. I do long to live in your presence. I want to be a woman who follows closely after you. Show me how I can sit at your feet, ready to learn. God, you have promised me that when I seek you with my whole heart, I will most certainly find you. I know that when I do, I will have joy, security, and satisfaction as well.

The one thing I ask of the LORD—the thing I seek most— is to live in the house of the LORD all the days of my life, delighting in the LORD's perfections and meditating in his Temple. PSALM 27:4

☀ **A prayer about PERFECTION**
When I don't measure up

HEAVENLY FATHER,

It is so easy for me to fall into the pattern of trying to be the best at everything I do. I want to be the best mother, the best wife, the best daughter, the best Christian . . . the list goes on and on. The problem with wanting to be the best is that the goal is unattainable. There are so many different ways to define being the best that I will never measure up to everything I think the world wants me to be.

Thankfully, you have come and changed the game. You are not asking me to be perfect; you are asking me just to believe in you and trust you with my life. You have created me in your image. I am not a mistake. Remind me every day that I don't need to please anyone but you.

Obviously, I'm not trying to win the approval of people, but of God. If pleasing people were my goal, I would not be Christ's servant. GALATIANS 1:10

☼ **A prayer about FAMILY**
   When my heart feels full and blessed

LORD,

Often I bring my frustrations to you when I'm weary and feeling overloaded with family responsibilities. Today, though, I'm laying my full heart at your feet in gratitude. Thank you for this beautiful family you've allowed me to love! Please help me to live and mother in a way that is worthy of such a reward.

Children are a gift from the LORD; they are a reward from him.
PSALM 127:3

DAY 329 *Prayerful Moment*

☼ **A prayer about BLESSINGS**
   When I need to remember that obedience is rewarded

LORD,

It's often said that obedience brings blessing and disobedience brings heartache. Maybe the effects won't be evident right away, but those two truths are timeless and unchanging. Please impress upon my children the value of seeking your ways and following them. May they understand that the peace and salvation you offer are worth far more than any earthly riches.

If you look carefully into the perfect law that sets you free, and if you do what it says and don't forget what you heard, then God will bless you for doing it. JAMES 1:25

DAY 330

☼ A prayer about being AFRAID
When I need to replace fear with faith

FATHER,

I find myself lying in the darkness late into the night with a heart full of fear. I confess I am afraid of failure, afraid of what the future might hold, afraid of what others might think about me. Some days it's as if these feelings are keeping me locked away from becoming the woman I believe you are calling me to be. Other days this fear paralyzes me from making choices and decisions, which keeps me from moving forward in the relationships in my life.

Father, ransom me and rescue me from myself. I rejoice that even though my heart may question the reality of my adoption into your family, ultimately I belong to you. You have called me to be your daughter, and my eternal security is forever sure and guaranteed. Please break my bondage to fear and show me pathways to move forward toward faith.

Now, O Jacob, listen to the LORD who created you. O Israel, the one who formed you says, "Do not be afraid, for I have ransomed you. I have called you by name; you are mine."
ISAIAH 43:1

☼ A prayer about FAMILY
When ours is at odds

LORD,

Submit. Dare I pray for help with that word again? I feel as though all I do is give in to someone in this house. Crazy thing is, I think everyone else here feels the same way. Lord, you designed submission to apply to each of us for our good as a whole, so how did it turn into a negative concept? Submission is really a decisive, fully empowered way to live—that is, when it isn't abused. Jesus submitted to your will, and you ask the same of us in this family so we can thrive together.

Please impress on all of us that we need to prioritize what's best for each other so that we can live in peace. Help me set the tone to help others see how submission blesses. Soften us toward one another, open our eyes to see our own responsibilities in this, and show us the areas we need to work on. Thank you, Lord, for setting the example of healthy, functioning, mutual submission that leads to mutual blessing.

Submit to one another out of reverence for Christ.
EPHESIANS 5:21

☼ A prayer about BOUNDARIES
When I want to live in your freedom

FATHER GOD,

I teach my children to obey the boundaries I establish for them, but if I'm truly honest, I don't always like to obey your guidelines for me. Sometimes I wonder exactly where those boundaries fall. Christians have such varying degrees of belief in you, and equally as many opinions regarding how to live out real faith. Thank you for today's verse, which clarifies the whole concept of boundaries. I guess yours encircle everything that draws me to you and keep out those thoughts and habits that would pull me away to be a slave to something unholy. Is that right, Lord?

Please continue to work on my understanding of your Word and your ways. I need your help even with the basic first steps of desiring to live for you wholly. Thank you for calling me to closeness with you. Strengthen the bond between my kids and me that nurtures their desire to live for you as well. May they be attracted to the joy and freedom they see in me when I obey you. Thank you that the boundaries in your Word really lead to freedom.

Don't you realize that you become the slave of whatever you choose to obey? You can be a slave to sin, which leads to death, or you can choose to obey God, which leads to righteous living. ROMANS 6:16

DAY 333

☀ A prayer about ADVICE
When I am confused about whose counsel to listen to

LORD,

The world's chatter seems so loud today. From the TV to the radio to the web browser to the repairman and the grocery cashier, everyone is ready and willing to offer advice— and those are just the strangers I encountered! There's no way one person can have all the answers, and much of it sounds good when it really isn't. I certainly don't know everything when it comes to raising faithful, well-balanced kids. I often need advice to live wisely myself.

So today, Father, I praise you for your wisdom. You are all-wise, ever-faithful, and the embodiment of truth. You are thorough in your counsel, and I can trust that your Word holds the answers I need. When I soak up your wisdom in Scripture, I can rest assured that your Spirit will speak discernment and discretion to me. Thank you for those benefits. Thank you for your guidance that helps me to be the mother my kids need.

Oh, the joys of those who do not follow the advice of the wicked, or stand around with sinners, or join in with mockers. But they delight in the law of the LORD, meditating on it day and night. They are like trees planted along the riverbank, bearing fruit each season. Their leaves never wither, and they prosper in all they do. PSALM 1:1-3

⚙ **A prayer about TIME**
When I want to steward my days well

GOD,

Thank you for past visits with my children and grand-children. Life looks different from where I sit now. As a new mother, I wondered if I would have enough hours in the day to care for my needy toddlers. As a young mother, I was impatient and wanted time to move more quickly so we could achieve the next milestone. As a mother of adult children, I realize I cannot stop time. It has rushed by more quickly than I would have liked.

Now I know that everything has its season and time. You have ordained all these ordinary moments and have given us a lifetime of love and happiness. You were there in the difficult days. I sensed your presence in the midst of our noisy celebrations. God, you have never left us or forsaken our family. I am more aware of the preciousness of every moment in life. You knew how many days you had ordained for each member of our family before the creation of the world. Give me grace to steward the time you have given me for your glory.

God has made everything beautiful for its own time. He has planted eternity in the human heart, but even so, people cannot see the whole scope of God's work from beginning to end. ECCLESIASTES 3:11

❁ A prayer about PERSEVERANCE
When I am exasperated

LORD,

Like a child throwing a tantrum, I want to throw myself down on the ground and scream. I am frustrated and at the end of my rope. I need you to give me strength and endurance to continue running this race. Please be with me.

God blesses those who patiently endure testing and temptation. Afterward they will receive the crown of life that God has promised to those who love him.
JAMES 1:12

DAY 336 *Prayerful Moment*

❁ A prayer about CHURCH
When I want my children to love worshiping with others

LORD,

Among all the groups vying for my children's affections, help them prioritize your church. I ask that they would find role models there and that they would feel a part of the local body of believers. May they do their part to grow your Kingdom and share your love here on earth.

Let us think of ways to motivate one another to acts of love and good works. And let us not neglect our meeting together, as some people do, but encourage one another.
HEBREWS 10:24-25

☀ A prayer about PLANNING
When I need to order my days

GOD,

Time seems to slip through my fingers like sand. I never seem to have enough minutes or hours in the day to get my to-do list accomplished. This mad rush fills my heart with discouragement, and I feel perpetually overwhelmed. Yet you, God, created seconds, minutes, hours, days, and all the seasons. You are fully present and working your good pleasure in each of these periods of time.

God, teach me to "realize the brevity of life." Show me what it means to count the days and make them count for you. I long to be a mother who lives with intentionality because no one is promised more time in this life. I want to make my life count for you—my time, relationships, daily growth in grace, and memories. More than anything else, I want to be a wise woman, every day applying the truth of what I know. Please show me how my daily schedule can be a reflection of you, the one who is ordered, purposeful, and wise in all you do.

Teach us to realize the brevity of life, so that we may grow in wisdom. PSALM 90:12

☼ A prayer about HUMILITY
When I am puffing myself up

LORD,

I can be such a judgmental person. Whether I am judging the mother whose child is throwing a fit in the grocery store or becoming outraged at the mother who dropped her sick kid off at day care, I can spend way too much time thinking I am better than everyone else. I would hate for my child to judge others because of the way they look, but I find myself doing it silently in my head all of the time. Constantly criticizing others is an ugly trait that I don't want to pass on.

I need you to remind me that there is always a real person behind what I see. I need to humble myself and remember that I am not better than anyone else. Help me to use the opportunities you put in front of me to show your love and compassion rather than to justify my own judgmental spirit. Open my eyes to see others the way you see them so that I can show them your love and kindness.

Don't be selfish; don't try to impress others. Be humble, thinking of others as better than yourselves. Don't look out only for your own interests, but take an interest in others, too. PHILIPPIANS 2:3-4

☼ **A prayer about THANKFULNESS**
  When I struggle with ingratitude

JESUS,

As the celebration of your birth approaches, I find myself swept up into the greediness of our culture. I am always amazed at how fast we move from the gratefulness of Thanksgiving to the consumerism of Christmas. I walk the aisles of the store and am captivated by the glitz and glamour of material goods. I covet shiny new things and allow discontentment to eclipse my heart. Ungratefulness is a strong contagion, especially as it impacts our home life. Who will get the most presents or the biggest ones?

But you, dear Savior, are our preeminent gift. You fill our family with so much joy. Help us to be grateful for all your many provisions. In the busyness of this season, we have the opportunity to live in a countercultural way. May the attitude of gratitude be the very air I breathe. Please give me moments to impact my family and friends as my heart grows toward contentment with all you have provided. May my mouth be filled with praise of you alone, and may my actions demonstrate to a watching world that you, Christ Jesus, are truly enough.

Whatever you do or say, do it as a representative of the Lord Jesus, giving thanks through him to God the Father.
COLOSSIANS 3:17

❉ A prayer about MIRACLES
When I lose faith

LORD,

Too often I find myself feeling hopeless when faced with an unsolvable problem. Whether it is overwhelming financial circumstances, a chronic illness, or a failing marriage— I tend to despair rather than hope. I forget that you are a God of miracles. I try so hard to fix things on my own and within my own power. But you are there waiting, hoping I will turn to you. You can provide a financial windfall, healing, or a solution I haven't even considered. You are bigger than all of my problems and have the power to move mountains. I forget that you are the almighty God.

Open my eyes to the miracles that you perform every day. Show me how to see things as my children see them. They see the wonder of your majesty in the blooming flowers, the crashing waves, and the flash of lightning—things I take for granted. Remind me of your power in my life today and give me a renewed hope and faith.

"You don't have enough faith," Jesus told them. "I tell you the truth, if you had faith even as small as a mustard seed, you could say to this mountain, 'Move from here to there,' and it would move. Nothing would be impossible."

MATTHEW 17:20

☀ A prayer about MONEY
When I focus on the wrong things

LORD,

I can spend way too much of my time worrying about financial issues. The fear of not having enough or not using my money wisely can be terrifying. It seems as if the bills just keep coming in. I can become paralyzed and either waste money by buying things I don't need or hold tightly to the money I have and be unwilling to give to others. Neither of these attitudes is how you want me to use the resources you have blessed me with.

Help me to trust that you will provide for my needs. Remind me that everything I own ultimately belongs to you, and show me how to spend my resources for your glory. Grant me a generous heart that freely gives to those in need around me. Help me to build this value into my children so they can grow up to exemplify the gift of generosity. Thank you for providing for our needs every day.

Those who love money will never have enough. How meaningless to think that wealth brings true happiness! The more you have, the more people come to help you spend it. So what good is wealth—except perhaps to watch it slip through your fingers! ECCLESIASTES 5:10-11

✸ A prayer about SERVICE
When I am thankful for devoted friends

GOD,

I am so thankful for my faithful and devoted friends. Their generous acts of love and service overwhelm my heart. Because they have been sensitive to your promptings, you have used them to meet some of my greatest needs. Dear Lord, please give them an extra measure of your blessing for the many ways they have blessed me.

Love each other with genuine affection, and take delight in honoring each other.
ROMANS 12:10

DAY 343 *Prayerful Moment*

✸ A prayer about THOUGHTS
When I need to guard my mind

LORD,

Unnecessary and unprofitable thoughts clutter my mind. Replace my impure thoughts with untainted ones. Fix my thoughts on what is lovely and admirable. Focus my mind on praiseworthy things. Inspire me to think honorable and Christlike thoughts that please you.

Fix your thoughts on what is true, and honorable, and right, and pure, and lovely, and admirable. Think about things that are excellent and worthy of praise. PHILIPPIANS 4:8

☼ **A prayer about GRACE**
When I am grateful for God's kindness

LORD JESUS,

Watching my child run and hide when he disobeys reminds me how grateful I am for the gift of your grace. You see me and know everything I do, and yet you extend forgiveness without heaping shame on my head. Your example is why I can scoop up my child in my arms and love him despite his failures. Thank you for always loving me, always believing in me, and always walking with me through the mountains and valleys of my life. Thank you for loving me despite my flaws, and help me to extend that same grace to my child. May he learn to live in the freedom that comes from turning his sins and weaknesses over to you.

Three different times I begged the Lord to take it away. Each time he said, "My grace is all you need. My power works best in weakness." So now I am glad to boast about my weaknesses, so that the power of Christ can work through me. 2 CORINTHIANS 12:8-9

☼ A prayer about ENDURANCE
When I need perseverance

LORD,

This time I've really had enough. I know I've claimed that in the past, but now there's truly nothing left of me to give. But you tell me to keep going anyway. You tell me to walk in your strength. With all due respect, Father God, what does that even mean? I'm the one who has to keep breathing, moving forward, making it through each day, enduring this agony, watching those I love hurt. I can't do it anymore.

I'm putting this back on you where it belongs, God. I need you to show me your bigness. Awaken me anew to your identity as GOD. Be GOD for us—bigger than we've thought, bigger than we could ever need at our weakest and most needy. Jehovah, Yahweh, the Great I AM. You created heavens and stars and earth. You cause mountains to move, kingdoms to rise and tumble, people's plans to change, and little ones to find families. You are Savior, Healer, almighty Warrior, tender Comforter. And GOD. I can't endure without you as GOD right now. It's on you, as you always intended it to be.

God is my helper. The Lord keeps me alive!
PSALM 54:4

☀ A prayer about NEGLECT
When I ignore my own needs

HEAVENLY FATHER,

As a mother, I think a lot about my child's needs, health, happiness, and well-being. I spend so much time worrying about being a good mother that I often neglect my own health and my own needs. You care about me even more than I care for my own child, and you don't want me to run myself ragged. As they so often say on airplanes, I need to put on my own oxygen mask before putting one on my child. That can mean that sometimes I need to stop and figure out how I need to care for myself or allow you to care for me when things get challenging. If I fall apart under pressure, I will be no good to my child.

Help me learn to care for myself and find ways to get rest in stressful times. Give me your strength and energy today as I take care of myself so that I am refreshed and ready to give to my family.

Don't you realize that all of you together are the temple of God and that the Spirit of God lives in you? God will destroy anyone who destroys this temple. For God's temple is holy, and you are that temple.

I CORINTHIANS 3:16-17

☀ **A prayer about the CALL OF GOD**
  When I don't feel so spiritual

LORD,

"The call of God"? Let's be completely honest with each other. Oftentimes I don't know what the call of God means in my daily life. Your call during dishwashing? Getting the kids ready for school? Running errands, voicing my opinion during a board meeting, taking the dog out before bedtime?

Most everyday moments I don't feel grand enough to hear a formal call from you. But you already know that, don't you? Maybe that's why you made sure the story of Samuel's call made it into your Word. You woke him up out of a sound sleep—several times, no less—until you got his full attention. He didn't recognize your voice at first, but eventually he was clued in that the persistent words were yours. Please call me like that today. Do what it takes to get my attention. Whatever small or large tasks you have planned for me, please help me listen for you throughout this everyday life.

The LORD came and called as before, "Samuel! Samuel!"
And Samuel replied, "Speak, your servant is listening."
I SAMUEL 3:10

☼ **A prayer about DECISIONS**
When I need to nurture my child's confidence to choose well

LORD,

It's not easy to know when to loosen the reins and allow my child more decision-making freedom. I'm still responsible for her, even if she makes a choice that leads to trouble. Since I can't hold her hand forever, will you please help me instill her with confidence and the desire to make decisions that honor you? Help me to hold back when she needs to see herself handle a situation, and help me to offer well-timed assistance or insight when it's obvious she needs it.

Keep my eyes focused on the goal of raising a strong person who (1) isn't so sure of herself that she avoids your guidance and (2) feels confident that she is capable of listening to you and choosing well. Show her what her strengths and weaknesses are, and help her to keep a learner's heart. May her strengths help her lead with integrity and vision, and may her weaknesses allow her to better understand the weaknesses of others. Bless this child, Father, as we raise her to be a blessing to this world.

Care for the flock that God has entrusted to you . . . because you are eager to serve God. Don't lord it over the people assigned to your care, but lead them by your own good example. 1 PETER 5:2-3

☼ A prayer about HEALING
When I can't make it better

HEAVENLY FATHER,

It hurts so much to see my child suffering. I want so much to be able to take away the pain and make everything okay. Only you can bring healing. You are Jehovah Rapha, the God who heals. Please bring relief from the pain today.

I am the LORD who heals you. EXODUS 15:26

DAY 350 *Prayerful Moment*

☼ A prayer about EVIL
When I'm burdened by the world's sorrows

GOD,

I don't know how you stand all the evil in this world. Some people have never known joy or security in this life. But Lord, thank you that you plan to heal and rebuild and wipe from existence all heartache that comes from unholiness. The joy that awaits us is beyond imagining. In the meantime, show me how I can reflect your loving care to those around me who are hurting.

He will wipe every tear from their eyes, and there will be no more death or sorrow or crying or pain. All these things are gone forever. REVELATION 21:4

⚙ **A prayer about WORDS**
When I speak unkindly to my loved ones

FATHER,

I am crying this morning because of how poorly I treated my daughter as she rushed out to school. How could I say all those unkind words to her? I allowed the circumstances of my morning to color my perspective. I did not even tell her how much I love her, and now she is gone. I don't understand how such cruel words and loving words can come out of the same mouth. I know that everyone speaks and acts out of the overflow of the heart.

So please search my heart, Lord, and show me everything wicked and sinful that I need to confess. Forgive me for treating my daughter in a way that does not reflect how much you love both of us. I repent of failing to keep short accounts with you. I have allowed my frustrations and anger to seep out in my conversations with my family. I pray, Father, for an opportunity to make peace with my daughter this evening. I want to move toward her in humility and love. Restore our relationship to a loving and grace-filled end.

Blessing and cursing come pouring out of the same mouth. Surely, my brothers and sisters, this is not right!
JAMES 3:10

☼ **A prayer about ADVERSITY**
*When I want to encourage my children's
deeper growth*

GOD,

The older my kids get, the more they are waking up to the world's troubles. I've seen fear in their eyes when they hear stories of war, abuse, crime, disease, natural disasters, injustice, even political uncertainty. Some of those tales have hit close to home. How do I help my children deal with fear of adversity, God? Because you allow us room to make decisions, we inevitably will deal with wrongdoing—ours and others'. But God, you don't let pain go to waste when we look to you for help and empowering in the midst of it.

I cannot shelter my kids from some of sin's effects. Please give me wisdom to weigh their maturity level and how much awareness they can handle. Help them desire deeper growth and strength through you as they deal with strife. As they mature, grow my kids strong with life-changing faith to handle the future. You are glorified when we trust you and let your light shine through us. Make that true of my children, Lord. Awaken them to your purposes in allowing troubles, and bring beauty from what may appear as disaster.

When your faith is tested, your endurance has a chance to grow. So let it grow, for when your endurance is fully developed, you will be perfect and complete, needing nothing. JAMES 1:3-4

☀ **A prayer about SPIRITUAL DISCIPLINES**
When I need to develop holy habits

LORD,

I feel as though you are testing me and trying my faith. I sense your purifying fires. Through prayer, I am realizing more and more how much I am trusting in myself rather than in you and your divine provision. Through your Word this week, I have been convicted about areas in which I am not aligning with your truth. In silence you have met me in love and flooded my heart with a desire to show compassion to others.

Thank you, Lord, for refining me and allowing the dross of my sinful behaviors to rise to the surface. Lord, I know I need to meet with you so I can know and serve you. These spiritual disciplines have served as a lifeline in the past. Give me grace to follow the holy practices you have shown me that are for my growth in grace. Nurture in me the habit of daily time at your feet so that I might become the woman you are calling me to be.

I will bring that group through the fire and make them pure. I will refine them like silver and purify them like gold. They will call on my name, and I will answer them. I will say, "These are my people," and they will say, "The LORD is our God." ZECHARIAH 13:9

☼ **A prayer about THANKFULNESS**
When I am grateful

LORD JESUS,

There is nothing like the sound of a child's laughter to remind me, even during the darkest times, that there is hope. I think you created that sound just for that purpose. It is easy for me to get down when things get hard. I can get discouraged and be tempted to think that you have forgotten me. But you have not promised me a life of ease. In your Word, you acknowledge that in this life, I will have trouble. But it is only for a season.

If I put my trust in you, you promise to be my rock and my refuge. This is the source of my hope and the origin of true joy. Remind me again today to be grateful for this promise and thankful for the blessings you have given me. Help me learn to rejoice in these promises today.

I pray that God, the source of hope, will fill you completely with joy and peace because you trust in him. Then you will overflow with confident hope through the power of the Holy Spirit. ROMANS 15:13

☀ A prayer about WORTH
When I am far too easily pleased

GOD,

I have spent far too many years chasing after virtually worthless life-plans. I am weary of trying to control my own destiny, and I see the futility of investing my life for temporal gains. Lord, please change my perspective from temporal to eternal. What will I profit if I chase after and gain the things of this world but forfeit my very soul?

I am precious to you—so treasured, in fact, that you sent your own precious Son to redeem my soul from a Christless eternity. I am forever grateful for this indescribable sacrifice on my behalf. Strengthen my children to resist the world's seductions, which threaten to move them away from godly pursuits. I know that only two things are eternal: God's Word and people's souls. Let my life be a testimony that stands as a singular quest toward investment in these priceless things. May I joyfully pursue heaven's treasure.

What do you benefit if you gain the whole world but lose your own soul? Is anything worth more than your soul?
MATTHEW 16:26

☼ A prayer about MARRIAGE
When I think about my child's future

LORD,

Though it may be many years away, I want my children to experience godly, healthy marriages. Help my husband and me to model such a relationship today. Please help me to prepare them for a long and happy marriage. I pray, too, that you would be at work even now in the lives of their spouses.

Since they are no longer two but one, let no one split apart what God has joined together. MATTHEW 19:6

DAY 357 *Prayerful Moment*

☼ A prayer about PLEASURE
When I want what I want

GOD,

Why do I always want what I want instead of what you want for me? My desire to be satisfied in these lesser things drives me further away from you than I ever imagined I could be. Give me strength to turn from worldly pleasures and find my greatest fulfillment in you.

We are instructed to turn from godless living and sinful pleasures. We should live in this evil world with wisdom, righteousness, and devotion to God. TITUS 2:12

※ **A prayer about ABILITIES**
   When I need a reminder of your strengthening

LORD,

My heart wants to tackle everything and never appear ruffled, to be known for getting the job done without wasting a breath on anxiety—and to look fabulous every step of the way. But many days I'm tested to the limit. Before I had children, I felt capable, efficient. I enjoyed being organized and on top of things. What happened to that woman? Now my patience and self-esteem falter when demands strike like bullets. I'm not Crafty Christy or PTA President Patty or Soccer Mom Sandra. Some mornings my children barely grab lunch money before racing to school ahead of the tardy bell. And my organized brain? If something isn't written down, forget it. Even my physical appearance shouts "Comfy Mom" instead of "Style Maven."

God, please refocus me so that your view of me shines through my countenance. Remind me that, with you, I'm able to handle what you allow me to face. I may not be a perfect mother, but my kids know they have my heart, and that's what matters most. Maybe my limitations are actually gifts when they nudge me to lean more fully on you.

I can do everything through Christ, who gives me strength.
PHILIPPIANS 4:13

☼ A prayer about GOD'S WISDOM
When I need discernment and guidance

LORD,

My husband and I are trying to make a final decision today as to whether or not we should move. We have loved being part of this community and raising our children here. We need your wisdom and discernment to navigate this process. We know many good reasons to go and many to stay. We know that whatever decision we make, the end result will impact our family.

Ultimately we want to be in the place where we can most strategically serve you as a family. You provide all the resources, such as time and money, regardless of the offer of a new salary. We come before you humbly as a family, asking you to direct our steps to the center of your will. May we model for our children what godly decision-making involves. Please show us clearly what choice to make by clearly opening and closing doors. We rest securely in the belief that you will faithfully lead us to where we need to be.

If you need wisdom, ask our generous God, and he will give it to you. He will not rebuke you for asking. JAMES 1:5

⚙ **A prayer about VICTORY**
When I need to stand strong in adversity

GOD,

I am weary tonight as I fall into my chair. I feel as if I'm encircled by fiery darts and have a target on my back. So many days I find that standing strong in the face of adversity is a difficult challenge. God, I know you have given our son to us and that he is a perfect complement to our family. His disability is an occasion to trust you daily, every minute. Each day I struggle just to get forward momentum. Communication and small motor skills are only possible through your gracious enabling.

Help me to see the small victories that occur every day. Forgive me for taking for granted all that you provide, such as finances for therapy and friends who encourage us along the way. Give me grace when my son is excluded from school or community activities because of physical or emotional limitations. Help me to remember that you are with us every step of this journey. Victory is found as we trust in your steadfast love.

The LORD your God is going with you! He will fight for you against your enemies, and he will give you victory!
DEUTERONOMY 20:4

DAY 361

☀ **A prayer about HOPE**
When my child is suffering

LORD,

Having to stand by as my child experiences pain is one of the hardest things I have ever had to endure. I want to swoop in and take the discomfort away. I think this must be how you feel as you watch your creation agonize in this sin-filled world.

I am so thankful that although this world is full of adversity and hardship, it is only a temporary dwelling place. You have given us hope in a future of living with you in a place where there is no suffering and no pain. I long for the day when I am able to live in paradise with you. In the meantime, please give my child comfort during this time of difficulty. Walk with us each day and help us to give our burdens over to you. Be present with us today.

We know that all creation has been groaning as in the pains of childbirth right up to the present time. And we believers also groan, even though we have the Holy Spirit within us as a foretaste of future glory, for we long for our bodies to be released from sin and suffering. We, too, wait with eager hope for the day when God will give us our full rights as his adopted children, including the new bodies he has promised us. ROMANS 8:22-23

☼ A prayer about GENTLENESS
When I need to model Jesus' tenderness

LORD JESUS,

When I see my children being inconsiderate while playing, I remind them to consider one another's feelings. I have lost count of the number of times I have asked them to share and play nicely. So why is it so difficult for me to see when I am doing the same thing? I can be unkind and inconsiderate to those around me when I am tired and frustrated. I don't always like to share my time and attention. I don't think everyone would always describe my actions as modeling the gentleness I desire to see in my children.

Lord, I confess to you my lack of consideration and ask that you help me cultivate more thoughtfulness in my life, not only with my children but also with relatives, friends, and others I encounter throughout the day. Thank you for modeling gentleness to me, and help me to be more like you.

They must not slander anyone and must avoid quarreling. Instead, they should be gentle and show true humility to everyone. TITUS 3:2

❖ A prayer about PURPOSE
  When I think my plan is the best

LORD,

Forgive me for my many agendas and plans that have little or nothing to do with the advancement of your Kingdom. Too often I assume that if I just bring my to-do list to you in my morning prayer, you will put your stamp of approval on my proposals. Lord, in your kindness replace my list with your perfect purposes for my life.

You can make many plans, but the LORD's purpose will prevail. PROVERBS 19:21

DAY 364 *Prayerful Moment*

❖ A prayer about PEACE
  When I am panicking

LORD,

Today I need your peace that transcends my understanding. My mind is racing, and anxiety threatens to overwhelm me. Fill me with your peace and calm my heart. Remind me that you are with me always.

I have told you all this so that you may have peace in me. Here on earth you will have many trials and sorrows. But take heart, because I have overcome the world.
JOHN 16:33

☼ **A prayer about PURITY**
When I want to live a transparent life

HOLY SPIRIT,

You see to the depths of my heart. I cannot hide from you. You see all my actions and all my hidden attitudes. You see beyond the exterior to the underlying motives, thoughts, and intentions of my soul. I long to live a transparent and authentic life, one that is visible to those around me. I want to live a life that is pure.

Holy Spirit, I know that when my heart is pure before you, then it will overflow with understanding, patience, kindness, and love. I need you, Holy Spirit, to reveal areas in my thoughts, words, and deeds that are impure and tainted. Help me to live in such close communion with you that I am quick to repent when my life is becoming contaminated by sin and wicked goals. I want you to cleanse all my impurities until I am whiter than snow.

We prove ourselves by our purity, our understanding, our patience, our kindness, by the Holy Spirit within us, and by our sincere love. 2 CORINTHIANS 6:6

TOPICAL INDEX